# Shares Made Simple

## A beginner's guide to the stock market

Rodney Hobson

HARRIMAN HOUSE LTD

3A Penns Road
Petersfield
Hampshire
GU32 2EW
GREAT BRITAIN

Tel: +44 (0)1730 233870
Fax: +44 (0)1730 233880
Email: enquiries@harriman-house.com
Website: www.harriman-house.com

First edition published in Great Britain in 2007 by Harriman House.
This second edition published 2012.
Copyright © Harriman House Ltd

The right of Rodney Hobson to be identified as Author has been asserted in accordance
with the Copyright, Designs and Patents Act 1988.

ISBN: 978-0857192-35-6

\*\*\*\*\*

British Library Cataloguing in Publication Data
A CIP catalogue record for this book can be obtained from the British Library.

Printed and Bound in Great Britain by;
Marston Book Services Limited, Oxfordshire

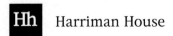 Harriman House

# Disclaimer

All the many case studies included in this book refer to genuine announcements and events on the London Stock Exchange. However, they represent the situation at each company referred to at a given moment in time. Circumstances change and issues raised at one juncture may be resolved or superseded. Similarly, new challenges arise over time.

Therefore nothing in this book constitutes a recommendation to buy or sell shares in a specific company or sector. Investors must exercise their own judgement, which they should be able to do with the aid of this guide.

Readers interested in finding out more about a particular company should read the latest stock market announcements and visit the company website.

At the time of writing the author held shares in Royal Dutch Shell, Barratt Developments and GlaxoSmithKline but not in any other company mentioned. These investments were being held for the long term.

# eBook edition

As a buyer of the print edition of *Shares Made Simple* you can now download the eBook edition free of charge to read on an eBook reader, your smartphone or your computer. Simply go to:

**http://ebooks.harriman-house.com/sms2**

or point your smartphone at the QRC below.

You can then register and download your eBook copy of the book.

# www.harriman-house.com

# About the author

Rodney Hobson is an experienced financial journalist who has held senior editorial positions with publications in the UK and Asia. Among posts he has held are News Editor for the Business section of *The Times*, Business Editor of the *Singapore Monitor*, Deputy Business Editor of the *Far Eastern Economic Review*, Head of News at Citywire, Editor of *Shares* magazine and Editor of the Hemscott financial website. He has also contributed to the *Daily Mail*, the *Independent* and *Business Franchise* Magazine.

Rodney is a speaker on investment issues, having appeared at the World Money Show and the London Money Show. He runs a seminar for beginners and less sophisticated share buyers each year at the London Investor Show.

He is registered as a Representative with the Financial Services Authority.

He is the author of four other books also published by Harriman House: *Small Companies, Big Profits*, a guide to investing in smaller companies, *Understanding Company News*, which explains company announcements and press reports, and *How to Build a Share Portfolio* and *The Dividend Investor,* both of which help private investors to pick suitable and profitable investments.

Rodney is married with one daughter.

Other books by the same author can be found at:

**www.harriman-house.com/thedividendinvestor**

**www.harriman-house.com/smallcompaniesbigprofits**

**www.harriman-house.com/understandingcompanynews**

**www.harriman-house.com/howtobuildashareportfolio**

Rodney Hobson's personal website is **www.rodneyhobson.co.uk**.

To Judy

# Contents

# Preface

## Who this book is for

This book has been written for those who are new to stock market investment or who want to broaden and deepen their knowledge of how the stock market works.

Anyone wishing to make their own investment decisions, rather than hand their assets over to a fund manager or see them stagnate in bank and building society accounts, will benefit from this carefully crafted step by step guide.

Even people with little spare cash but who want to be informed of the financial world we live in can gain a greater understanding of how the City of London and other business centres operate.

The book is also an invaluable tool for anyone who professionally needs to know about the stock market, from potential wheeler-dealers to advisers such as auditors and PR, to back office staff and students on business or media courses.

## Structure of the book

The book is organised to take readers logically through the various stages of understanding stock market investment, with each new concept explained in simple terms as it arises.

It begins by outlining what shares are, why they exist and why people buy them, followed by a look at the London Stock Exchange and what it is there for.

We discuss how to make sensible decisions on which companies to invest in, sifting the mine of information that is published through the stock exchange, and learn how to pick out the key points in company results, including the warning signs.

With the basics explained, it is time to look at how to buy and sell shares, where to get advice and how to remain well informed.

Finally, we look at takeovers and mergers, the most exciting aspect of stock market investing and the area that offers most scope for making money to investors who, like those who have read this book, understand what is going on.

## Supporting website

The accompanying website for the book can be found at:
**www.harriman-house.com/sharesmadesimple2**

# Introduction

When I sat down to start writing the first edition of this book early in 2007, the storm clouds of the sub-prime mortgage scandal, the credit crunch, global recession and the eurozone crisis were no more than specks on the distant horizon.

The FTSE 100 index looked set to top 7,000 points for the first time. Bank shares were pushing to new highs and those of the mighty Royal Bank of Scotland were heading for 500p. Two years later the FTSE 100 plunged below 4,000 points and RBS shares were in single figures.

Yet this apparent catastrophe demonstrated how vital a simple but well-constructed share portfolio is for any investor. Those with even the most basic knowledge of the stock market and how it operates have come through the storm with enhanced assets. They easily avoided pitfalls such as clinging onto shares in Northern Rock or Bradford & Bingley until they were worthless.

Millions of new, unsophisticated investors were lured into joining the great share-owning democracy, first by the privatisation issues and then by the conversion of building societies into banks. They set off hopefully, looking for their share of the elusive gold that paves the City of London, the nation's financial heart, but with only the vaguest notion of what shares are, what they are for or what to do with them.

I know this is true from the many phone calls I received on the City desks of *The Times* and the *Daily Mail* from baffled readers who binned vital documents from companies they held shares in because they did not have a clue what they were being told or what vital decisions they needed to make.

So I wrote a long overdue book to put that right and now, five years on, it is time to update the content and to provide up-to-date examples of the points that are explained, such as:

- What the stock market is and how it works.

- Why share prices go up and down.

- Why some companies look cheap while others appear to be expensive.

- How to make money and avoid heavy losses.

- The traps that snare the unwary.

By reading this book, you will find that the finance pages of your daily newspaper become a mine of information instead of a daunting mist of incomprehensible murkiness.

You can, if you wish, turn straight to Section D and take a direct leap into the exciting and lucrative world of stock market investing. Or you can use the index to treat this book as a reference work.

However, I would urge all new investors and those with little experience to be patient. Learn to walk before you can run. Start at the beginning and be led logically, step by step, through an easy-to-follow guide to those gold-paved streets. All the baffling issues are dealt with clearly and simply.

I cannot pick your shares for you but I can tell you what to look for and how to look for it. Above all, I will endeavour to provide a level playing field in a world still dominated by professional players as you seek your share of the nation's wealth.

*Rodney Hobson*
*April 2012*

# SECTION A
## Shares

# Chapter 1
## What Are Shares?

If you are going to invest through the stock market, we had better start with what it is that you are actually buying.

You will be buying what are known as ordinary shares. You, together with all the other investors who have bought shares in a particular company, will become the owners of that company. You have a right to a say in the decision making and you share the profits through the payment of dividends.

These shares are often referred to as equities. They represent ownership of the company, just as you have equity in your house: the percentage of your house that you own when the building society's loan is deducted.

The names of the shareholders and the number of shares held will be kept on a share register. Each time a batch of shares changes hands, the new shareholder will be recorded on the register.

### There is a difference between running a company and owning it

The day-to-day running of the company will be carried out by a board of directors who may act as if they own the company but they do not. It is you, and the other shareholders, who are the owners. The directors do have the right to own shares. Indeed it is normal for them to buy shares as a show of faith in the company they are running. They have exactly the same rights as shareholders as you do.

Shareholders have the right to attend an annual meeting where they can question the executives who run the company, to receive accounts at least twice a year and to vote for who will be the directors and who will be the auditors. They can approve or veto any proposed major acquisition of another company or the proposed sale of a major part of the existing business.

The number of votes you have and the size of your share of the profits depend on how many shares you own. If you have 1,000 shares in Marks & Spencer and someone else has 10,000 shares then they have 10 times as many votes as you do and they will receive 10 times as much in dividends. Every share carries one equal vote.

## Stocks or shares?

In the United Kingdom the two terms stocks and shares have become virtually synonymous but the terms shares and shareholders are normally used, so these are the terms that will be used in this book.

The Americans tend to refer to stocks but they are talking about the same thing as our shares.

Each share has a nominal value. This was the value of each share when the company was originally formed.

If you have a penny black stamp in your possession, it was originally issued back in 1840 for 1p. That is its face value, not its value today. It can be sold for whatever a stamp collector is prepared to pay for it. Similarly you should not expect to pay the nominal face value of a share. You have to pay whatever price the share commands on the stock market.

## Where do shares come from?

In the first instance, shares are issued by the company when it is set up. Investors put money in to get the company going. Premises have to be bought or rented, machinery may be needed, staff have to be paid, materials bought ... all this before any money comes in from customers. In return, the investors are allocated a stake in the company.

Money, or capital as it is referred to, is one of the many inputs that a company needs. Capital can come through the founders putting their hands in their pockets, from taking out bank loans or from selling shares.

The issuing of new shares by the company is known as the primary market because it is the first time that the shares have been allocated to investors. When these shares are subsequently bought and sold on the stock market, that is the secondary market.

Think of it this way. When a builder puts up a house and sells it for the first time, this is the primary market. When the house is sold on to new owners, that is the secondary market. It is exactly the same with shares.

We shall discuss the primary and secondary markets in chapter two.

## Issued capital

How many shares a company issues is decided by the company itself. There is no fixed number of shares. The number of shares will depend basically on how much capital the company has needed to raise, not only when it was first set up but also at any time subsequently.

The shares that have actually been sold by the company to shareholders are the *issued share capital* (this is also referred to as the *called-up capital*).

Do not expect a conveniently round number. For example, high street retailer Marks and Spencer in its 2011 annual report had an issued capital of 1,584,863,882 shares.

## Part paid shares

When you buy shares you will almost invariably have to pay up the full amount due immediately but on very rare occasions you may pay for the shares in instalments.

5

Investors who bought shares in the privatisation issues, when the government was selling off state enterprises, may recall that in some cases payments to the government were made in instalments; the idea being that more ordinary investors would be tempted to join the great share owning democracy if they could pay in manageable bits, just like buying a washing machine in monthly instalments.

This is a very messy and expensive arrangement, since some shareholders inevitably forget by the time the third payment is due or they simply do not have the cash. Either way they have to be chased up, which is why part payments rarely happen.

## A and B shares

We have assumed so far that you will be buying ordinary shares and that these will rank equally with each other. Each ordinary share has one equal stake in the company and one equal vote.

There is one exception to this, and that is where there are two classes of ordinary shares known as A shares and B shares.

In the past, some family-owned companies tried to get the best of both worlds, raising cash by selling shares but retaining family ownership by the rather sneaky method of having two classes of shares. One class of shares, usually the A shares, had one vote each and were sold to the general public while the other class, usually the B shares, had 10 votes each and were issued to the family.

Thankfully this subterfuge is now regarded as unethical and has all but disappeared. The best known name that still treats the public unfairly with two classes of shares is that bastion of moral rectitude, newspaper publisher Daily Mail & General Trust. Its A shares, the ones most widely traded on the stock market, have no votes although there are nearly 400 million of them, while the 20 million ordinary shares control the company. Technically you can also buy the ordinary shares on the stock market but don't bother looking for them; they are rarely traded and just two shareholders held 88.8% of them according to the 2011 annual report.

A and B shares used to be widespread in the brewing industry and two examples survive, though not to the detriment of ordinary shareholders. Youngs A shares with full voting rights are the ones traded on the stock market and not the ordinary non-voting shares; Fullers A shares, also with full rights, are the ones that are traded and not the B shares with only a tenth of a vote each.

Royal Dutch Shell has A and B shares but these have equal rights and the split exists only because Shell is an Anglo-Dutch company. The A shares are for Dutch investors and the B shares for those in the UK.

During privatisations you may have come across the Government's golden share, which was the ultimate B share. The Government hung on to one share in each privatised company, which could be used to outvote all the other shares put together. This golden share was retained in case the Government felt it needed to intervene in the national interest. Golden shares were used in the UK as a veto only twice and the European Court of Justice has ruled that they are against European law unless national interest is clearly at risk. They can now be disregarded.

## Preference shares

There is one other class of shares apart from ordinary shares and they are called preference shares. These are in fact more like loans than shares. Preference shareholders do not have voting rights except on issues that specifically affect them. They receive a set rate of interest, usually twice a year, just as you would receive a rate of interest on a savings account in a bank or building society.

It is possible to buy and sell preference shares on the London Stock Exchange in the same way that you buy and sell ordinary shares, although not all companies issue preference shares. Dividends on preference shares must be paid before dividends on ordinary shares and if the company goes bust any cash left over when the creditors have been paid off goes to the preference shareholders first. That's why they are called preference shares.

However, we naturally hope that our investments have gone into prosperous enterprises. While the poor preference shareholders are stuck with a fixed rate of interest, we, the ordinary shareholders, see our dividends rising along with the profits of the company.

As we shall see throughout this book, investors who take the greatest risk expect to receive the greatest reward, and this does tend to happen although there are no guarantees.

## Convertibles

Companies raise money by taking out loans, usually by borrowing from the bank through overdrafts or term loans, which are loans for a set number of years. They may also borrow from the general public by issuing loan stock, also referred to as bonds, in much the same way that shares are issued except that holders of loan stock do not own the company.

Some loans can be converted into ordinary shares. These loans are known as convertibles.

The terms on which they can be converted, and the dates at which conversion is allowed, will have been set out when the loans were issued. If the loans are at any time converted into ordinary shares, these shares will carry exactly the same rights as those of existing ordinary shares.

Preference shares may be convertible into ordinary shares and will thus be convertible preference shares.

# Chapter 2
## How Shares Are Created

## Primary market

The primary market is the creation and sale of new shares. Most of the time you will be buying second-hand shares but we will look first at the different ways in which new shares may be issued to the public.

By the 'public' we do not just mean small investors like yourself or wealthy individuals. Shares are also held by large institutions such as pension funds. We shall refer to these as institutional investors.

### Initial public offerings

When a company decides that it wants to raise money by issuing shares to the public for the first time it will make what is called an initial public offering (more usually referred to by the initials IPO).

This is also dubbed as *coming to market* or a *flotation*.

The shares may be new ones created by the company, in which case any money you spend in buying them will go to the company to be used in expanding the business.

Alternatively, the existing owners may be looking to cash in on their success and are offering some of their shares for sale. In that case, the cash goes to them. The owners may be the people who set up and built the company from scratch and they now want to enjoy the fruits of their labour. It could be a family firm with no-one in the next generation wanting to inherit the business.

Quite often an IPO is a mixture of new shares sold on behalf of the company and a batch of shares from the existing owners.

A prospectus giving all relevant details is issued before an IPO takes place. It will state how many shares are being issued, who the directors are and their history and whether there are any skeletons in the cupboard such as outstanding law suits.

Any investor seeking to buy shares in an IPO can contact the company and request a prospectus, although IPO shares are often issued only to institutional and large investors because it is cheaper and simpler than seeking out a large number of small investors.

It is possible in an IPO that the existing owners intend to retain a certain number of shares. The prospectus will spell this out. It will also indicate if the owners have given an undertaking not to sell any or all of their remaining stakes for a specific period of time. This will alert you to the possible danger that a large slab of shares could be dumped onto the market at some future date, depressing the share price.

Companies that have come to market in the past may create new shares in addition to those issued in the IPO. Sometimes, as in the issue of vendor shares or share options, existing shareholders are not directly affected and no action is required.

## Vendor shares

When a company makes an acquisition, in other words it buys another company, it may pay cash but it may alternatively pay partly or entirely in its own shares. These are new shares issued to the owners of the company that is being bought, the vendors. You will have come across the term vendor, the Latin word for seller, if you have ever bought a house.

Often the vendor will give an undertaking not to sell any of the shares for a set period of time. Alternatively, the vendor may place the shares immediately with institutional investors or keep them as a long term investment.

## Share options

The directors and other key executives may be awarded share options, which means they have the right to buy a set number of shares at a set price. Share option schemes are designed to provide an incentive to management.

The price the managers have to pay to buy the shares is fixed, often at quite a cheap price, so they can pocket a profit by buying the shares cheaply and selling them at a higher price. The better the company is doing, the more the shares will be worth and the bigger the profit the managers can make on their options.

Buying shares in this way is called exercising the options.

## Other ways of creating new shares

There are other occasions when companies already listed on the stock market may create more shares:

- **Rights issues.** Existing shareholders are given the right to buy more shares at a set price

- **Placings.** New shareholders are given the opportunity to buy shares at a set price. Placings may also include the right for existing shareholders to participate

- **Bonus issues.** Existing shareholders are given extra shares free in proportion to their holdings

- **Share splits.** Each existing share is divided into two or more shares.

I will deal in greater detail with these share issues, explaining the implications for shareholders and what action if any needs to be taken, in chapter twenty.

## Secondary market

We have seen that there are various ways in which new shares are created but for the most part you will be buying shares on the secondary market, that is buying existing shares second hand. You will do this through the stock market, which we will be looking at in Section B.

It is quite likely that all the shares you ever buy will be bought on the secondary market. Certainly all the shares you ever sell will be sold on the secondary market.

The cash you pay for these shares does not go to the company. It goes to the person who already owns the shares. When you sell any shares you own, the proceeds of the sale come to you, not to the company.

## Share cancellations

Shares can be cancelled as well as created. When a company is taken over, the new owners often buy all the shares from the existing shareholders and scrap the lot.

Less dramatic is the growing trend for companies to buy back some of their shares. This happens when a company has spare cash that is not needed for investment in the business. This process is often referred to as returning cash to shareholders, as it is the reverse of the process we have discussed in the primary market where the company issues shares to investors to raise cash.

Shares are also cancelled in a share consolidation, a process that almost invariably means that the shares have sunk so low in value that they are hardly worth buying. For example, when a share price falls below the level of 1p the mechanisms for trading shares can become quite impracticable.

Say the consolidation is one share to replace every ten you already own. The hope is that the one share you now own will be priced at ten times as much as each of the shares you previously held.

Unfortunately shareholders often take the opportunity of a share consolidation to sell out, so the price tends to settle below the theoretical price. Hopefully, after reading this book you will be sufficiently competent at investing to be able to avoid such companies.

## Treasury shares

Occasionally a company may buy its own shares cheaply in the hope of reissuing them later at a higher price. While these shares are held in abeyance they are known as treasury shares.

# Chapter 3
## Whose Company Is It?

The company is owned by the shareholders. Your stake in the company is in proportion to the number of shares you hold. So if you own 5% of the company you are entitled to 5% of the votes at any shareholders' meeting and also to 5% of any profit distributed as dividends.

The company will employ a firm of registrars to keep the register of shareholders up-to-date, amending the list as shares are bought and sold and mailing out the annual report and any other information that shareholders are entitled to receive.

In practice, most companies have institutional investors such as pension funds on their shareholder register and their holdings will be considerably larger than yours. They will, when things go wrong, make known their disquiet to the directors and although it may seem a little unfair that their voice is louder than yours, in most cases your interests and those of the institutions will be the same.

The directors may also sound out the views of large shareholders on a major issue such as a change of strategy or a major acquisition. It can be useful to know if a planned course of action is going to run into serious opposition.

However, companies are not allowed to give crucial information to favoured shareholders without also releasing that information to everyone through a stock exchange announcement.

The London Stock Exchange has, over the years, made valiant efforts to stamp out the issuing of inside information and the flow of information today is much, much fairer than it used to be.

## Shareholder revolts

The company is run on behalf of the shareholders by a board of directors. In practice, the directors tend to have a pretty free rein and, in some cases, can come to regard the company as their personal property. If it comes to a vote, though, they can be ousted by the shareholders and occasionally, though very rarely, this does happen.

Case study: BSkyB

One of the most high-profile cases of a shareholder revolt against a director occurred at British Sky Broadcasting, where James Murdoch was installed as chairman by his father, the media mogul Rupert Murdoch.

The Murdoch family controlled News Corp, the largest single shareholder in BSkyB with 39% of the shares. Discontent over the family's prominent position in the British media had rumbled on for years, as had concern over their political influence.

Matters came to a head when News Corp made an offer to buy all the BSkyB shares that it did not already own. The bid was pitched at 700p, which was above the prevailing stock market price but well below the 850p that shareholders felt News Corp should and would be prepared to pay as long as the independent members of the BSkyB board put up a fight, which they did.

The fight lasted long enough for the *News of the World* and *The Sun* to become increasingly embroiled in the phone hacking scandal and, although he had not been in charge of the newspaper division when the hacking happened, James Murdoch also became tainted by the allegations. After a year of getting nowhere, the Murdochs abandoned the bid.

BSkyB shareholders staged a revolt when James Murdoch subsequently came up for re-election as their chairman.

Although 81% of shares were voted in his favour, closer analysis of the figures showed that nearly half of the non-News Corp votes cast were either against him or were abstentions.

Murdoch finally resigned as chairman of BSkyB in April 2012.

Shareholder revolts naturally tend to coalesce around annual general meetings, when the shareholders vote on a whole range of issues including the election and re-election of directors.

Most revolts tend to be over executive pay schemes, especially in the aftermath of the banking crisis when there was public outrage over bonuses. These usually fizzle out ahead of the meeting because if there is sufficient disquiet among large shareholders the board will usually back down and avoid the humiliation of losing a vote.

Companies that have amended pay schemes in the face of protests include: luxury clothing retailer Burberry, media agency WPP, bookmaker William Hill, software group Misys and stationery and newspaper retailer WHSmith.

## Directors

Directors may hold shares in the company. Indeed, it is considered rather bad form if they do not as it looks like a vote of no confidence in themselves if they are not prepared to risk some of their own money in buying at least a nominal stake.

There is no set figure for how many shares a director should hold. Sometimes the entire board will hold less than 1% between them. Sometimes just one director holds more than half the shares. Factors that can affect the size of directors' shareholdings include the size of the company and whether a director has a residual holding from the days before the company was floated on the stock exchange.

## Example: directors' shareholdings

As examples of directors' shareholdings, the two tables show one company where the board's holdings add up to less than 1% of the total shareholding and another where one director owns more than half the shares.

Chemring is a medium sized company supplying defence equipment such as decoys, flares and ammunition. On 2 March 2012, shareholdings of directors were:

Table 1: shareholdings of Chemring directors

| Director | Position | Holding (shares) | Percentage of company (%) |
|---|---|---|---|
| David Price | Chief executive | 650,795 | 0.336 |
| Paul Rayner | Finance director | 220,000 | 0.114 |
| Peter Hickson | Chairman | 90,000 | 0.047 |
| Sarah Ellard | Company secretary | 75,587 | 0.039 |
| David Evans | Non-executive | 75,000 | 0.038 |
| Sir Peter Norriss | Non-executive | 28,000 | 0.014 |
| Ian Much | Non-executive | 26,500 | 0.013 |
| Lord Roger Freeman | Non-executive | 1,750 | Less than 0.001 |

Source: Morningstar

Terrace Hill is a small property company that develops housing and commercial sites and owns offices and shopping centres as an investment. In March 2012 its directors' shareholdings were:

Table 2: shareholdings of Terrace Hill directors

| Director | Position | Holding (shares) | Percentage of company (%) |
|---|---|---|---|
| Robert Adair | Chairman | 131,241,239 | 61.915 |
| Philip Leech | Chief executive officer | 2,039,447 | 0.962 |
| Bob Dyson | Non-executive | 623,000 | 0.294 |
| Jonathan Austen | Finance director | 180,000 | 0.085 |

Source: Morningstar

Any shares held by directors count equally with those held by other shareholders. A director with 5% of the shares has 5% of the votes, just as you would do with a similar stake.

There are two types of directors: executives and non-executives. They tend to sit on the board in roughly equal numbers but there is no set formula for how many of each a company should have.

## Executive directors

The executives work for the company full-time and are responsible for the day-to-day operations. The most important executive is usually called the chief executive, or group chief executive or chief executive officer (CEO for short). In a smaller, privately owned company they would probably have the title managing director.

Whatever the actual title, this person is the top executive, the one to whom the other executives report.

After the chief executive the most prominent executive is usually the finance director. Other executives who may be on the board include the sales director, the marketing director and the heads of each division in the group. There will also be a company secretary who carries out certain defined legal roles. This is not always a separate post. The role could be fulfilled by, say, the finance director if the company is not large enough to justify a separate appointment.

## Non-executive directors

The non-executives are part-time and may do no more than attend monthly board meetings. They are there to represent the interest of the shareholders – people like yourself. They are usually chosen for their wide business experience and their role is to offer advice and to see that the executives are doing their job.

They will probably be non-executives of several quoted companies, though they should not sit on the boards of two rival companies as there would be a clear clash of interests. They can, though, facilitate contact between two companies in which they are directors if there is a mutual advantage.

The chairman of the company is normally, though not always, a non-executive. He or she may well have an office at the company and perhaps work two or three days a week there, offering help and guidance to the executives as required. This is regarded as a highly prestigious post.

The chairman chairs the board meetings, just as the chairman or woman of any formal organisation such as the Women's Institute or the British Legion does. He or she sees that the agenda is followed, that the meeting is orderly, that all directors have their fair say and that important issues are addressed.

There is also a vice-chairman who is also usually non-executive and who deputises in the absence of the chairman.

The top two roles on the board are chairman and chief executive. It is regarded in the City as best practice for two separate people to hold these two roles with the chairman as a non-executive. In the past it has been common, when a chairman retires or resigns, for the chief executive to step up to the chairman's role and a new chief executive to be appointed. Such a move has the advantage of ensuring that the new chairman is very familiar with the business and how it operates.

This practice has, however, become increasingly frowned on, the argument being that an outsider is completely independent while the newly promoted former chief executive is too cosy with the other executives and may persist in interfering with the day-to-day running of the company.

Occasionally one person holds both posts, which puts a great deal of power into one pair of hands. We also sometimes see an executive chairman as well as a chief executive. This can cause problems over who does what and is likely to create a conflict between rival egos.

There is some kind of pecking order on the board, partly in terms of each individual's role in the company and, in the case of non-executives, based on length of service on the board.

However, it is inevitable that other factors come into play in determining whose voice carries most weight. As in all walks of life, some individuals are more ambitious than others, some are more forceful.

The importance of a balanced board was amply demonstrated at Royal Bank of Scotland, where the independent directors failed to rein in chief executive Fred Goodwin, whose expansionist policies finally overstretched the bank to the point where it collapsed into a government bailout in the financial crisis.

A chief executive who is demonstrating success in the business will command more respect than one running a struggling enterprise. Some non-executives are more adept or daring in controlling a maverick executive. Directors, in the end, are only human. Some boards pull together and others split into factions.

## Directors' pay

Deciding how much the directors are paid for their services is a particularly contentious area. The board will set up a remuneration committee, probably comprising three non-executives and chaired by the longest serving one.

Executive directors will be paid for doing a full-time job, possibly quite handsomely, and there are likely to be incentives such as bonuses if certain performance targets are met. Performance targets may involve meeting minimum profit levels or raising the value of the shares on the stock market by a certain percentage.

Executives are often awarded share options, where they are allowed to buy new shares from the company cheaply or even at no cost. They will also have generous payments made into their pension fund.

Non-executives are normally paid a fixed, much lower fee, reflecting the fact that they may do no more than attend a monthly board meeting. The chairman's salary will depend on how much time he is required to spend on company business.

As a general rule, the bigger the company, the higher the remuneration for directors.

As noted earlier, the shareholders can object to the salary structure at the annual meeting but it is extremely difficult to persuade large shareholders to make a fuss.

# Chapter 4
## What's In It For Me?

You've invested your money and you naturally want something in return. There are three ways you can benefit from a stock market investment:

1. dividends

2. capital gains

3. shareholder perks

## Dividends

Most companies pay dividends, which come out of their profits. This is similar to receiving interest from a savings account in a bank. You get a flow of income without touching the capital invested.

If you want to invest for income, say you are retired and want to put your nest egg where it will provide you with a regular supply of cash to live on, then you will look for companies paying a dividend that is increased year by year. This is known as a *progressive dividend*.

Dividends are paid out of what are called distributable reserves. In simple terms, this is the pot of cash that has been built up out of the profits left over after all the bills have been paid, including tax and previous dividends.

The cash that is not distributed to shareholders in the form of a dividend is used to pay off debt, meet day-to-day bills or to fund expansion.

## Dividend cover

Companies generally aim to cover the dividend twice. That means that in any year they hope to earn twice as much as they pay out in the dividend.

For example, supposing a company makes £100m in profits after tax. Let us also suppose that it has 200m shares in issue, so it has earned 50p for each share (called earnings per share). Say it pays a dividend of 20p a share. That means the dividend is covered 2.5 times by earnings – in other words earnings are two and a half times the dividend.

These figures are purely a simple illustration. In real life they hardly ever come out in round numbers, as we can see in the following table of actual examples. However, company results always include a figure for earnings per share and one for the dividend, so you can easily see whether the dividend is covered.

Table 3: sample earnings per share and dividend figures

| Company | Earnings after tax | No of shares | Earnings per share | Dividend total | Cover |
|---------|-------------------|--------------|-------------------|----------------|-------|
| Michael Page | £56.9m | 3,304.5m | 18.7p | 10p | 1.87 |
| BAT | £3,857m | 1,970m | 194.6p | 126.5p | 1.54 |
| Barclays | £3,007m | 11,988m | 25.1p | 6p | 4.18 |
| WPP | £840.1m | 1,260m | 67.6p | 24.6p | 2.75 |

Source: Company results announcements for calendar year 2011

We can see that dividend cover can vary considerably. This may be because of a blip in earnings or the result of a deliberate policy by the company concerned.

Tobacco company BAT is content with comparatively low cover because of its solid and rising earnings from a wide geographic spread of markets. Although it has been under fire in developed countries where the health risks of smoking are trumpeted, it has found new markets to replace any lost sales.

Recruitment specialist Michael Page is quite close to having earnings cover the dividend twice. Again, its global spread means it does not have to be overcautious as a downturn in one part of the world is likely to be offset by gains elsewhere.

Although marketing and advertising group WPP is the largest company of its kind in the world, it has taken a more conservative line given that media spending is more likely to fluctuate considerably and markets in the West had been subdued.

Finally Barclays Bank has unusually high coverage of its dividend. This is understandable given the traumatic events of the previous three years, in which Barclays narrowly escaped the government bailout that befell rivals Lloyds and RSB.

There are cases, alas, when the dividend is not fully covered. In this case the company has to raid the reserves built up in the fat years as it trades through the thin ones. This cannot be done for ever, because the reserves will dwindle and when they run out it will not be legally possible to pay out any more.

If the company chooses to maintain the dividend – to pay the same amount this year as it paid last year – even though the dividend is not fully covered, it is hoping to do better in future and to restore profits to a comfortable level.

## Dividends paid in instalments

Most companies in this country pay dividends twice a year:

- once after the half year end (the interim dividend), and
- once after the financial year end (the final dividend).

Add the two together and you have the total dividend for the year.

As a rough guide, about one third of the total is usually paid out at the half way stage and two thirds after the year end. There is no set formula for this division and you should not be suspicious if a company pays the two dividends in different proportions.

### Reasons for a smaller interim dividend

There are, though, two main reasons why the interim tends to be significantly less than the final.

Firstly, the company does not have a full picture of how well the year is going at the half way stage. After all, it has only half the year's figures to go on.

This is particularly true of companies that depend heavily on Christmas trading because in most cases the festive season falls in the second half of the financial year.

It is also true of holiday companies that run at a loss during the quieter winter period and make all their money in the summer sunshine. They tend to have a financial year end in September so the first half may give only a preliminary indication of how the full year will pan out. Who knows in March how many last minute bargain hunters will leap off their sofas to snap up cheap breaks?

The second reason for the smaller interim is more technical. Strictly speaking, the directors merely recommend the dividends: the payouts have to be approved by the shareholders at the annual general meeting.

You and your fellow shareholders are hardly likely to demand a smaller payout. So the directors pay the interim dividend reasonably safe in the knowledge that it will in the fullness of time be approved by the shareholders. There are no qualms about the final dividend because the annual meeting is called after the full year results are announced and the final dividend is not paid until that meeting gives the go ahead.

Just for the record, turkeys do on rare occasions vote for Christmas. There have been instances of a major shareholder arguing that it is in everyone's interest to preserve cash to develop the business for a long-term and, ultimately, a larger gain rather than pay out a smaller amount now.

### Paying more or fewer dividends

A few companies pay quarterly dividends. This happens more in the US than here but larger companies with an international standing, such as oil giants BP and Shell, pay out quarterly to keep their American investors happy. The three interim payments tend to be equal instalments and the final dividend may be larger but again there is no set formula for how the total is divided.

Some smaller companies pay only one, final dividend. It is obviously twice as expensive to mail out cheques two times a year rather than just once. It may be inconvenient to wait a whole 12 months for your dividend but there is no reason to suspect the soundness of such a company. Rather, it can be a cause for rejoicing that a company with limited resources uses them prudently.

Finally, we have companies that pay no dividend at all. These are obviously of no use to you if you are looking for a stream of income from your shares unless, perhaps, there are genuine reasons to believe that a dividend is imminent.

It is possible that the directors have decided to preserve cash to use in expanding the business. More likely is that the company is loss making or has no distributable reserves so it is in no position to pay a dividend.

We will concentrate on the companies of most interest, the ones making two or four payments a year.

## Dividend size

Whether payments are half-yearly or quarterly, the policy on how much to pay out at each stage remains much the same year by year at each individual company. So if the interim dividend is unchanged, it is unlikely that the final will be increased either.

On the other hand, if the interim is raised, then the company is clearly confident that the year is going well and the directors are expecting, barring any nasty surprises, to raise the final. So if the interim is raised, say, 5% you can hope that the final dividend will also go up

5%. This is not guaranteed, and indeed if everything goes swimmingly you might get even more, but if trading tails off in the second half you could be in for a disappointment.

Companies do occasionally rebalance the respective proportions of their dividends. For example, directors who have been extremely cautious in setting the interim dividend in the past may feel able after a few years of strong trading to increase the interim faster than the final over one or more years to bring the ratio into line with the norm.

When a company decides to rebalance the dividend it will say so in its results statement, usually before such a change is made or possibly to explain a large dividend increase that has just been recommended.

Successful companies will have a progressive dividend policy, that is, the dividend will be raised every year. This is great for investors because the rising payout will offset the effects of inflation.

Not so good is when companies 'rebase' their dividends. This is a euphemism for saying that the company is not making sufficient profits to justify the dividend at its current level. By setting a lower dividend for the latest financial year, the company hopes to be able to start a progressive dividend policy but from a lower level.

The following table shows a selection of dividends paid by companies of various sizes over a five year period. The figures are for the calendar year. We can see that dividends tend to rise in steady stages but they can fall sharply if profits suffer a serious setback.

Table 4: sample dividends paid over five years

| Company | Business | 2007 | 2008 | 2009 | 2010 | 2011 |
|---------|----------|------|------|------|------|------|
| Centrica | Oil & Gas | 11.57p | 12.63p | 12.8p | 14.3p | 15.4p |
| Devro | Food products | 4.45p | 4.45p | 5.0p | 7.0p | 8.0p |
| Amec | Engineering services | 13.4p | 15.4p | 17.7p | 26.5p | 30.5p |
| Cookson | Industrial materials | 19.58p | 5.85p | Nil | 11.5p | 21.75p |
| Persimmon | House building | 51.2p | 5.0p | Nil | 7.5p | 10p |

Source: company annual reports

Centrica provides the sort of pattern we are looking for as investors: steadily rising dividends year by year. Devro also looks promisingly on the move after holding its dividend unchanged for one year. Amec is even better, for the dividend has not only been rising but gathering momentum.

Cookson and Persimmon both slumped in the middle of the period but at least Cookson has got back quickly to where it was at the start. Persimmon is back on the right track but is way short of its halcyon days.

### Dividend currency

The dividend will be declared in pence per share, in euros per share if the company is based in the Republic of Ireland, or in US cents in the case of some international companies, particularly those in the oil industry. Very rarely, some other foreign currency may be used such as the Australian dollar.

If a foreign currency is used, the dividend will be converted into sterling at the prevailing exchange rate before it is paid to you.

## Special dividend

Occasionally a company will pay a special dividend. This is usually much bigger than the interim or final. It happens when a company suddenly finds itself with more cash than it can use and the directors decide to return it to shareholders rather than leave it to gather dust in a bank account.

One instance is when a company sells a major business to another company for cash. Another possibility is that the company has been very successful and has built up a cash pile over the years. Eventually the directors realise that they do not need to set so much aside for a rainy day.

A special dividend will usually be in addition to the interim and final dividends. This is so that the special dividend is clearly seen as a one-off. You cannot expect another special dividend in the following year.

## Payment dates

When a dividend is announced the company will set two dates:

1 **Qualifying date.** Shareholders on the share register on this date are entitled to receive the dividend

2 **Payment date.** This is the date on which payment is transferred to your bank account through the BACS system or the dividend cheque is sent out.

There is no set timeframe for dividend payments. Some companies pay within a few weeks of declaring the dividend; others wait months.

Up to the qualifying date the shares will be bought and sold cum dividend. That means with the dividend. If you sell shares at this stage the right to receive the dividend passes to the buyer.

Ultimately the day arrives when the company pays up and the shares go *ex dividend*, that is without the dividend. (You learn Latin reading this book as well as maths!) Now you keep the dividend if you sell the shares and you are not entitled to it if you buy the shares.

When shares go ex dividend, the price will fall to reflect the fact that the buyer will not get the payout. This fall will be roughly equivalent to the size of the dividend.

Five large companies went ex dividend on Wednesday, 15 February 2012. The following table shows the size of the dividend paid and the movement in the share price that day.

Table 5: effect of going ex dividend

| Company | Dividend | Share price change | Effective change |
|---------|----------|--------------------|------------------|
| Royal Dutch Shell | 30p | -30p | - |
| Unilever | 18.79p | -25p | -6.21p |
| AstraZeneca | 123.6p | -119.5p | + 4.1p |
| GlaxoSmithKline | 21p | -19p | + 2p |
| Rank | 1.1p | + 0.5p | + 1.6p |

Shares were generally little changed that day, with the FTSE 100 index losing just 7.1 points, so we would have expected the shares to fall by roughly the value of the dividend.

Oil company Shell did exactly as expected in falling by the same amount as the dividend but the others in our list did not fit the pattern. Household goods supplier Unilever saw its shares fall by noticeably more than the dividend. Pharmaceutical giants Astra and Glaxo eased back by less than the dividend. Rank fared best of all, with its share price rising despite the shares going ex dividend.

Note: The dates of dividend payments can usually be found in the 'investor relations' section of companies' websites.

## Capital gains

You may be more interested in seeing the value of your shares rise than in receiving a steady stream of income. In that case you will be looking for companies that you feel are undervalued by other investors and whose share prices will rise as other investors catch on. You want to get in first.

The money you invest is referred to as capital and any increase in its value is a capital gain.

## Having it both ways

You can have the best of both worlds by investing in companies that see their share prices rise as the dividend goes up. In fact, you may ask, surely the two go together.

Indeed, you may see an ideal investment as one where the profits rise year by year, the dividend paid out of those profits similarly rises, making the shares more attractive, so more investors want to buy and the share price goes up further.

Quite right. Profits, dividends and share prices often do move in the same direction in roughly equal measure.

Do remember, though, that the stock market rarely moves in symmetrical ways. Some companies may pay more out in dividends while others retain the cash for expansion. A company that has made heavy losses in the past may seem a worthwhile investment now it is making profits but it may have no reserves left to pay a dividend.

# Shareholder perks

A minority of companies offer shareholders discounts off their products or services. These include jewellery, clothing, food and drink, air fares, new and used cars and magazines.

For example, Eurotunnel offered its original shareholders three free trips through the Chunnel each year, while various housebuilders have offered thousands of pounds off one of their new homes.

These perks can look very attractive but there are several disadvantages:

1. Most obviously, if you do not want to travel by car to France or buy a new home from a particular builder then the concession is of no use to you. There is no point in buying shares at Moss Bros if you get your suits at Marks & Spencer.

2.  A minimum shareholding is often required to qualify for the perk. Although in some companies just one share is sufficient, others reserve the benefit for holders of at least 2,500 shares.

3.  Companies may require investors to hold the shares for a minimum period, usually one year but sometimes longer.

4.  Perks can be withdrawn or changed so it is difficult to keep track of what is currently available. Some companies notify the shareholders about what perks are offered in the annual report so you have to buy the shares first and find out your entitlement later.

When you are paid cash as a dividend you can spend the money as you please. But with perks you are stuck with what you are given.

The following table shows a selection of the perks that have been, and may still be, available but investors will need to check with individual companies to ensure that the concessions still exist.

Table 6: sample companies and perks offered to shareholders

| Company | Sector | Perk | Minimum shareholding |
| --- | --- | --- | --- |
| Mothercare | Retail | 10% discount up to £50 | 500 shares |
| Bellway | House builder | £625 off every £25,000 spent | 2,000 shares held for 1 year |
| Thomas Cook | Travel | 10% discount off holidays | No minimum |
| Signet | Jewellers | 10% discount | No minimum |

The most comprehensive list of company perks is collated by the stockbroker Hargreaves Lansdown and is available free on its website at: **www.h-l.co.uk/free-guides/shareholder-perks**

An alternative source is Barclays Stockbrokers: **www.stockbrokers.barclays.co.uk/content/ads/documents/Shareholder_Brochure.pdf**

# Chapter 5
## Is My Investment Safe?

Imagine walking into a bookmakers and finding that most horses won, often at pretty decent odds. Or visiting a casino where there is no zero on the roulette wheel and the dealer's blackjack cards are dealt face up.

Welcome to the world of the stock market.

Yes, it is a gamble picking shares but it is one where the odds are stacked in favour of the punters, where the majority walk out winners instead of losers.

Shares do arguably represent a riskier investment than putting your money into a savings account with a fixed rate of interest but the risk is much less than you think and the potential rewards are much greater.

During the credit crunch some savings accounts looked quite risky, which is why queues formed outside Northern Rock as worried savers rushed to withdraw their cash and why the Government of the Republic of Ireland stepped in to guarantee all savings in Irish banks. Banks in Iceland did in fact go bust.

Sure, if you put away a large enough sum of money into a savings account you might be able to live off the interest – for now. But your savings are being eaten away all the time by inflation. As the years go by, that fixed rate of interest is worth less and less while your lump sum never increases.

By contrast, dividends on shares generally rise over the years to offset inflation and, over time, most shares increase in value.

## Minimising risk

Every investor needs a well balanced portfolio of about 10-12 shares spread across different sectors such as a bank, a house builder, a power company, a transport provider and so on. So if one share suffers, the likelihood is that the others will compensate.

Yes, it is possible for the whole market to tumble, as it did between 2000 and 2003, but even if you bought right at the top of the market in March 2000 and clung on obstinately you would still probably be better off today than if you had let your cash dwindle away in the bank or building society.

In that sense, investing in the stock market is safer than a savings account. And you can decide for yourself how much risk you want to take. Do you go for big solid household names or pick out up-and-coming young companies? By learning how the market operates and how to avoid pitfalls you can learn to take sensible decisions to create a portfolio that suits you.

It is true that there are unscrupulous people in the stock market as there are in any walk of life. Shares often move before a big announcement as those in the know buy or sell before the rest of the market catches on. Insider trading is virtually impossible to stamp out entirely.

However, there are three different bodies policing UK stock market investments with considerable effect:

1 London Stock Exchange,

2 Takeover Panel, and

3 Financial Services Authority,

Let's look at these three in some more detail.

## 1. London Stock Exchange (LSE)

First, there is the London Stock Exchange. It has strict rules on when directors can buy or sell shares in their own company and on when they must alert the market to a change in profit expectations. All formal announcements on matters such as takeovers and mergers, results and major transactions must be made publicly at the earliest opportunity. In practice, such statements are almost invariably issued through the London Stock Exchange itself.

We shall be looking more closely at the role of the LSE in the next chapter.

## 2. Takeover Panel

Then there is the Takeover Panel, whose job is to ensure fair play not only in takeovers but also in mergers and when large investors take major stakes in a company. The Panel oversees the Takeover Code, which sets a timetable for bids, decides when control has passed to a new owner and determines what the various parties to a bid can say and do.

Above all, the Panel ensures as far as possible that all shareholders great and small must be treated equally in a takeover. The Panel has, over the years, tightened the rules on takeovers to level out the playing field and is not afraid to take on big guns in the financial world to do so. It has built a reputation for being fair to all participants and for enforcing the rules where necessary.

We shall look in more detail at takeovers in section E.

## 3. Financial Services Authority (FSA)

Finally, until April 2013, the Financial Services Authority has an overall responsibility for regulating the entire financial services sector, including stock market dealings. It can investigate suspicious trades and fine companies and individuals who do not play the game.

Ordinary private shareholders are not directly affected by the FSA, whose role is mainly keeping an eye on investment professionals.

The Conservatives included in their 2010 general election manifesto a commitment to return some of the FSA's powers to the Bank of England. This will be done by splitting the FSA into:

- The Prudential Regulation Authority, which will be part of the BoE and will take charge of banking supervision
- The Financial Conduct Authority, which will be the consumer watchdog

However, in the final resort it is up to you to go into stock market investing with your eyes open, to do your homework and to know what you are doing. Do not expect some fairy godmother to step forward and make up your losses. After all, you expect to pocket any gains you make, so pay up if you get it wrong. The stock market is not for wimps.

## Shares versus other investments

Other forms of investment apart from savings accounts can make you money. Gold has on occasions proved a good short term bet. Rare stamps, paintings, coins, wine, even carpets have their day. Indeed, in the past tulip bulbs presented one of Europe's most notorious boom and bust stories.

As with your house, with shares, with the contents of your attic, what you own is worth what someone else is prepared to pay. And if the price of a case of 1996 Latour or an 1882 British Empire Orange stamp starts to motor then other investors are sucked in until the bubble bursts.

Stocks, too, can be subject to the vagaries of passing whims, as first biotechs and then computer technology shares have demonstrated in recent years. The big safeguard with shares is that unless you take silly risks on ephemeral fancies you are buying a stake in something that has a real value of its own in addition to the price that another investor is prepared to pay for it. For as long as the goods the company makes or the services it provides have value, then the company and its shares have intrinsic value.

Shares are linked to the health of UK and overseas economies. The amount of goods and services sold rises as economies grow and falls in recession. The fact is that economies around the world spend longer growing than contracting. The world is, overall, a richer place than it was 10, 20, 50 or 100 years ago.

By investing in shares, you take your stake in the increasing wealth of the UK and the world.

If inflation is only 2.5%, then £10,000 falls in value to £9,750 over the course of just one year and to £8,810 in five years. If inflation is 5%, then your £10,000 is halved in less than 15 years. So you have to constantly top up your savings account out of the interest you receive just to maintain the real value of your savings. It is like running to stand still.

Shares on average not only keep pace with inflation, they provide you with an income as well.

There have been periods when shares have fallen over several months, even over years. The FTSE lost three quarters of its value in 1973-74. In 2000 we launched on a decline that was not quite so steep – the FTSE 100 lost over half its value – but it was a much longer downward grind lasting three years.

However, shares gain in value in far more years than they fall.

## Shares v gold

Chart 1: UK stock market compared to gold

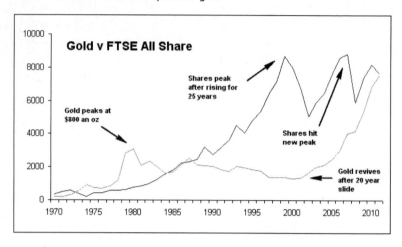

The chart shows the general performance of the UK stock market since 1970 – with, for comparison, the performance of gold over the same period. It tells us which is the genuine safe haven, gold or shares.

The stock market suffered what seemed at the time a serious setback when oil prices quadrupled in 1973-4. Around that time the gold price, which had been pegged to the US dollar, was set free so it zoomed from around $150 to $800 in pretty short order.

Yet this outperformance by gold proved short-lived. As the gold price subsided for 20 (yes, 20!) years shares powered ahead, opening up a massive gap over gold. Despite the much heralded surge in the price of gold since the year 2000, and despite two serious setbacks on the stock market, all gold has done in a dozen years is to almost close the gap.

*And* this does not take into account the fact that gold produces no income while shareholders have had 50 years of steadily rising dividends.

### Shares v property

The one other alternative form of investment that combines income with rising values is property. There has over the past few years been a boom in buy-to-let, purchasing houses to rent out. As with shares, values can fall as well as rise but they rise more years than they fall.

Property does involve administration and maintenance. While you can decline to commit more cash to your portfolio when money is tight, you cannot ignore a leaky roof whether you have the cash to fix it or not.

## Insider trading

The use of privileged information to gain an advantage in the stock market is pernicious and will be impossible to stamp out entirely as long as greed is one of the seven deadly sins.

Too many people within a company or among its advisers are party to information ahead of an announcement of events, such as results or a takeover bid, for the authorities to ascertain where any leak came from; especially when the culprits give hints to friends and relatives who do the actual trading.

The London Stock Exchange does routinely investigate any unusual or sharp movements in share prices and any surge in trading volume, especially in companies that subsequently reveal price-sensitive information. The Financial Services Authority has launched criminal prosecutions, though with limited success.

While this is a matter for concern, we need to get it in proportion. Unless you bought shares just before a takeover approach was revealed, or intended to buy shares but were put off by the share price increase, you have not been affected adversely. Only those who paid over the odds for their shares or who missed out on a short term profit have cause to complain.

If you already held the shares, then you benefited from the share price increase.

Because companies are obliged to issue a public statement when there is a sharp movement in their share price, we are talking about a very short time frame, possibly just the first hour of trading when most private investors are inactive. Once the news is out in the open, the shares would rise anyway.

## The Takeover Code

Companies that have received a takeover approach are expected to do the decent thing and inform the market as soon as there is any reasonable prospect of a firm offer emerging.

However, the Takeover Code explicitly acknowledges the obvious fact that a company may not be aware that it is being eyed up as a bid target and it cannot be expected to disclose something it does not know about yet.

Nor do companies need to reveal every single conversation they have with a potential bidder. One might argue that all approaches should be revealed immediately but that would be quite impracticable and would do more harm than good.

Many approaches come to nothing so there is no point in boosting bid hopes prematurely. As it is, many approaches are rejected without being translated into a firm proposal or the potential bidder decides it is not worth pressing its case.

However, target companies are required to do the decent thing and own up if their share price starts to rise while secret talks are going on to nip any insider trading in the bud. Changes to the Takeover Code in 2011 increased the onus on target companies to confirm or deny rumours.

Insider trading can also happen ahead of the announcement of better or worse than expected company results. Here the authorities have been much more successful in stamping out the insider trading that was once widespread.

Companies have become far more responsible in keeping investors informed of any changes in trading conditions and they are certainly required to alert the stock market to any substantial changes in profit expectations, whether for better or worse.

We shall look at takeovers in more detail in section E.

# SECTION B
# The Stock Market

# Chapter 6
## The Market Place

The stock market, like any market, is where you buy and sell new and second hand goods, in this case shares in a company. Companies willingly pay a fee for a stock market listing because it is easier to persuade investors to buy shares if they can be sold easily at a later date.

Shares do not have to be traded on a stock market. Supposing you have a bright idea but you do not have the cash needed to make and market the wonderful gizmo that you have invented. You ask your Grandma, or Auntie Maisie, or the neighbours, anyone who believes in you to put up the cash in return for a stake in the rewards when your great invention starts to sell like hot cakes.

Alas, Grandma dies, you fall out with Auntie Maisie and your neighbours move to the Outer Hebrides and the cash has to be repaid just when you need it most. Wouldn't it be so much better if new investors stepped forward to buy the stakes of those who want out? If your shares are traded on the stock market, that is exactly what happens.

What is more, people will be far more willing to put their faith and their life savings into your venture if they have the reassurance of knowing that, should they want to get out, they can do so readily.

The stock market provides the reassurance that it will bring together buyers and sellers on a trading platform where the price of the transaction will be set according to supply and demand.

## The London Stock Exchange

The main exchange for trading shares in this country is the London Stock Exchange (LSE). Although Antwerp can claim to be the first city in which share trading took place on a large scale, London led the way in adopting a set of share trading rules and as such was the first formal stock exchange. It remains one of the three most prestigious in the world alongside the New York Stock Exchange in the US and the Tokyo Stock Exchange in Japan.

Because these three exchanges are in different time zones, it means that from the opening in Tokyo to the close in New York there is a major stock market open somewhere for most hours of most weekdays.

In addition to UK companies, over 300 overseas companies from more than 50 countries have their share prices quoted on the LSE to gain access to the finance they need to flourish.

The total number of companies quoted on the LSE is well over 2,000 and they are worth in total more than £2,000 billion.

A London listing gives these companies from across the globe prestige. They are attracted by the liquidity of the London market and the balance that we have here between encouraging entrepreneurial spirit and imposing sufficient sensible regulation to retain the confidence of investors and quoted companies alike.

Liquidity refers to how active the market is. The more buyers and sellers there are for a company's shares, and the more trading that takes place, the more liquid those shares are. They flow readily. If trading is active, investors are willing to buy because they know they will have no difficulty in selling whenever they want to.

## History of the Exchange

The London Stock Exchange began with brokers meeting in London coffee houses way back in the 18th century. Indeed, it can be argued that the issuing of a list of stock and commodity prices in 1698 is the earliest evidence of organised stock market trading in the world.

The dealers had to meet in coffee houses at first because their behaviour was too rowdy for the liking of the Royal Exchange, where other commodities were traded.

The first stock exchange premises were established in 1761 and when formal membership, by subscription, was instituted in 1801, the modern stock exchange where members could trade with each other was born. Eleven years later a rule book was created.

It took until 1973 for the first female members to be admitted and in the same year the regional stock exchanges that had sprung up in cities beginning with Manchester and Liverpool were amalgamated into one national exchange.

## Big Bang

Since then modernisation has snowballed in the electronic age. Deregulation of the market, known as Big Bang, took place in 1986.

Until then, trading had been a highly complex business full of restrictive practices such as being able to charge investors minimum rates of commission. Although investors placed their buy and sell orders with stockbrokers, these orders had to be relayed to jobbers on the stock exchange floor. Errors could occur as jobbers misunderstood each other's orders or scribbled down the wrong details in the hurly-burly of the trading floor.

Everything had to be matched up at the end of the day and disputes were settled by an independent committee.

Brokers and, in particular, the jobbers who saw their jobs disappearing, forecast that Big Bang would be the end of the world but in many ways it was the start of the LSE as we now know it.

All member firms became broker-dealers, able to take orders and do the actual buying and selling. Minimum commission rates were abolished, so private investors were encouraged to place orders because they now paid lower charges.

The old octagonal stock exchange building was situated just round the corner from the Bank of England in the main part of London's financial centre known as the City. It used to be buzzing with brokers, jobbers, traders and investors.

Now trading is carried out mostly on silent computer screens in offices scattered around the globe rather than face to face on a market floor and the LSE has moved into smaller new headquarters in Paternoster Square close to St Paul's Cathedral.

The Stock Exchange Electronic Trading Service (SETS) has been established to make trading instantaneous and CREST, an automatic settlement service, clears shares and payments electronically without the need for paper.

The London Stock Exchange used to be owned by its members, such as stockbrokers. It is now owned by shareholders and its shares are traded on the exchange just like those of any other company.

## Trading hours

The London Stock Exchange operates within set hours. At 7am the formal announcements lodged overnight while the exchange was closed start to pour out. The intention is to give everyone an equal opportunity to trade on a fair basis. Announcements will continue to be made throughout the day but the overwhelming majority come out as the market opens.

In theory we therefore all start trading on an equal footing. Yes, the professionals in the City are going to be at their desks and ahead of the average punter first thing in a morning so you will, in practice, find that share prices often move before you have a chance to react. However, at least there is some attempt to create a level playing field.

Trading in smaller shares starts at 7am. Those in larger companies do not start until 8pm, after the London Stock Exchange has run a complex computer program through to match up any attempted trades left over from the previous night.

Trading then continues right through the lunch hour until 4.30pm.

Announcements continue to be issued until 6.30pm. Most after-hours statements cover directors' share dealings but occasionally a profit warning is slipped out, perhaps in the hope that the press won't notice. (The press always do notice and in consequence this underhand practice is far less common than it used to be.)

Table 7: summary of London Stock Exchange trading hours

| Time | Event |
|------|-------|
| 7am | Trading in smaller shares starts<br>Formal news announcements start |
| 8am | Trading in main shares starts |
| 4.30pm | Close of trading |
| 6.30pm | Formal news announcements end |

### News announcements

The overwhelming majority of announcements are made through the London Stock Exchange's Regulatory News Service (RNS). This used to be compulsory but other news distributors are now allowed to compete provided they make the information widely available to newspapers, to wire services such as the Press Association and to financial news websites. The aim is to spread the news to all investors as widely and quickly as possible.

News that has not been released in this way does sometimes leak out into the newspapers. The powers that be discourage this practice. In particular, the 'Friday night drop' in which financial advisers slipped out tasty morsels to favoured Sunday newspaper journalists after the market had closed for the week has been stamped out.

However, where news genuinely occurs after the stock market has closed, it is permissible for companies to release the information to the press provided at least two newspapers or news agencies such as the Press Association or Reuters are informed.

Curiously, the tipping off of scribes on the *Financial Times*, the newspaper read by City professionals on their way to the office, has never been attacked by financial regulators with the same zeal as leaks to lesser publications.

Do not be too angry that the professionals have a built in advantage. Share prices can be erratic first thing in a morning and unsuspecting private investors who instruct their stockbrokers to buy or sell at the best available price as soon as the market opens often strike a worse deal than they expect.

If you miss an opportunity, learn to live with it and move on. There are plenty more investments to be made.

# Chapter 7
## Full Listings And AIM

The London Stock Exchange (LSE) does not have the right to a monopoly on share trading in the UK, although it has been, since its inception, by far the largest stock exchange in the country.

Indeed, in the past there were several stock exchanges in large cities around the UK. Since the millennium international banks made a concerted attempt to set up a serious rival and looked at one point as if they would succeed but the venture failed for lack of liquidity. The main competition today comes from Plus, formerly known as Ofex (because trading was off the London Stock Exchange). This market is not part of the LSE and the regulations governing companies whose shares are quoted on Plus are less rigorous. It tends to cater for very small, comparatively new companies.

All companies whose shares are traded on the LSE market are known as quoted companies (alternatively it can be said that they have a stock market quotation).

There are two sections to the LSE: the main board and the Alternative Investment Market (AIM). Strictly speaking only companies on the main board are 'listed', that is they appear on a list of companies that comply fully with LSE regulations and financial reporting requirements, although the term is now widely used to also describe AIM companies.

## Full listing

Most of the biggest companies in the country, and many foreign ones, have their shares traded on what is known as the main board (even if share prices are no longer stuck up on a board in a trading room in the exchange).

This is referred to as a full listing. Listed companies must abide by certain rules which are designed to protect investors, such as:

- Newly listed companies must have a record of trading successfully for the previous five years.

- Listed companies must issue financial results twice a year within a set time and a trading statement every quarter.

- They must issue a warning if profits are likely to fall substantially short of expectations, or alert investors if they are doing considerably better than anyone thought likely.

- Directors are allowed to buy or sell shares in their own company only at specified times when all relevant news is known to everyone. They cannot, for example, trade just before results are announced – the close period – or when they know that any information that could influence the price of their shares is to be issued.

- Companies must hold an annual meeting at which all shareholders are entitled to attend.

The LSE charges companies a fee for the right to have shares listed on the main board. While this is no problem to giants such as BP or Vodafone, the cost can be onerous for smaller companies. Also there may be worthy companies that fall a little way short of the requirements for a full listing.

So the LSE runs a second trading board called the Alternative Investment Market (usually referred to by its initials AIM).

## Alternative Investment Market

AIM has been an amazing success story since it was established in 1995 with just a handful of companies traded and it has attracted more than 1,000 companies whose shares were worth about £70bn in aggregate at the start of 2012.

The fees are lower on AIM than for a full listing so it is ideal for newer, growing businesses. The rules are laxer, and although they still offer some protection to shareholders you should be aware that investing in AIM companies carries a greater risk than for the main board.

In particular, there has been controversy over whether companies based in Eastern European countries with a different legal system to ours should be allowed in and whether there are sufficient safeguards when a single shareholder or a few acting together own more than half the shares.

Some companies want their shares to be quoted on AIM in the hope that one day they will grow up and join the big boys on the main board, as Domino's Pizza for example has done (they joined AIM in 1999 and then transferred to the main market in 2008).

Others, such as clothing retailers Asos and Mulberry or oil explorer Rockhopper, are happy to be quoted on AIM, although they have the size for a full listing if they so wished; while some companies such as biotech firm Renovo used to have a full listing but have moved to AIM for the looser regulation and/or to save money.

The chart below shows the performance of AIM stocks relative to stocks with a full listing – the greater volatility of the former can easily be seen.

Chart 2: AIM v FTSE All-Share Index

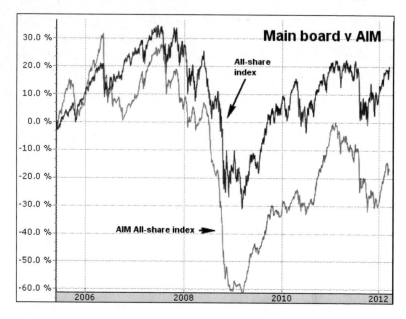

It is also clear that between 2005 and 2012 AIM stocks as a whole underperformed those on the main board. We will look at how indices are compiled and what they tell us in chapter nine.

Just as the main board is the premier stock market in Europe, AIM is the most prestigious market for smaller companies in Europe and it is rapidly gaining a worldwide reputation, attracting, among others, emerging Chinese companies anxious to raise Western capital to offset the lack of investment funds at home.

## Regulation

The requirements for a quotation on AIM are minimal. There is no minimum size for companies joining; no minimum percentage of shares that must be in public hands; no trading record is needed; and there is no requirement for companies to be incorporated in the UK.

However, the AIM market is not lawless. The complete set of rules can be found on the London Stock Exchange website at:

**http://www.londonstockexchange.com/companies-and-advisors/aim /advisers/rules/aim-rules-for-companies.pdf**

Approval of shareholders is not required for most transactions.

The one major requirement is that companies must have a nominated adviser (or nomad for short). The nomad must be approved by the LSE – the list runs to about 60 – and actually has to meet more requirements than the AIM-quoted company itself. The nomad is responsible to the exchange for assessing that the company is suitable for AIM and for advising and guiding the company on its responsibilities.

If an AIM company falls out with its nomad and suddenly finds itself without one the exchange will suspend trading in its shares. Failure to find a replacement nomad means expulsion from AIM.

AIM companies must also have a stockbroker to ensure that there is a market in the company's shares. The nomad usually acts as broker.

Although joining AIM may look easy, quoted companies are required to play fair, for example:

- They must inform shareholders, through the LSE, of any changes in their financial condition such as increasing their bank loans or failing to pay them when due.

- They must alert the market immediately if they realise that their business has taken a distinct turn for the better or for the worse and if profits are likely to beat expectations or to fall short.

- Any change in the nature of the business must be disclosed, including plans to acquire another company or to sell part of the existing business.

In short, an AIM company must speak up if it knows of anything not yet in the public domain that would substantially affect the share price when it leaks out.

The LSE has powers to discipline AIM companies that get out of line. It can issue a warning, a fine or a censure and, in the last resort, can throw the company out. Nomads tend to take these disciplinary actions as seriously as the companies they advise, since it affects their reputation.

AIM companies must publish their interim and full year results within four months of the period end.

Directors cannot buy or sell shares in their own company for up to two months before results are announced, or at any time when they are in possession of price sensitive information that has not yet been published. For example, they cannot dump some of their shares on the market when they know they are about to issue a profit warning.

### Inheritance tax

Most AIM stocks are exempt from inheritance tax after they have been held for two years. Those that do not are land and property; financial activities including banking and insurance; legal services and accountancy; farming and forestry; and managing hotels and nursing homes. The list could change at the whim of the Chancellor of the Exchequer.

This exemption is, admittedly, a benefit for your heirs rather than for you but it is worth remembering in these days when avoiding inheritance tax has become a national sport and all the other obvious loopholes have been closed by Chancellors of the Exchequer in successive Budgets.

Note that Gordon Brown hinted at the possible removal of this benefit when he raised the inheritance tax threshold in his 2007 Budget. Although he is no longer around at No. 11 Downing Street to withdraw the perk, the door has been opened for one of his successors to do so.

Already the Chancellor gets his revenge by refusing to let you put AIM stocks into ISAs or PEPs, the tax-free investment schemes.

This can be particularly inconvenient if you have in your ISA a main board company that decides to move down to AIM. If a company announces its intention to move down to AIM you are likely to see heavy selling, not only from ISA holders but also from investment funds that specifically invest only in full listings.

## Suspension of share trading

Companies can have trading of their shares suspended or even cancelled for breaches of rules, though the LSE is reluctant to take such drastic steps unless necessary as it punishes the innocent shareholders, who are then locked in to holding shares that cannot be sold, along with the errant directors.

The most likely reason for a suspension is a failure to produce interim or full year results within the specified time of four months.

Most companies failing this requirement tend to comply within days but longer suspensions have been known.

Examples of shares being suspended include:

- Shares in staffing agency **Healthcare Locums** were suspended early in early 2011 after it issued a profit warning and said that 'serious accounting irregularities' had been brought to the board's attention. Two senior executives were suspended. Trading in the shares did not resume until after a financial rescue the following September. AIM used to have a rule that any company suspended for six months was automatically removed permanently. Had that still been the case Healthcare Locums would have been delisted in July 2011.

- Founded by Beatle George Harrison, film company **HandMade** asked for its shares to be suspended in 2010 because of 'uncertainty in relation to the financial position'. It was its third suspension in three years. The announcement was prompted by AIM rules stating that companies must issue without delay notification of any change in financial position that could affect the share price.

- Caravan and mobile homes seller **Discover Leisure** went into administration in October 2011 and the shares were suspended. Attempts to raise additional funds to keep going had failed and the directors decided that the business was no longer a going concern. The assets were sold off.

We should note that companies can ask for trading in their shares to be suspended pending an important announcement. This may be a sizeable acquisition or possibly a takeover of the company.

Where the dreaded phrase 'pending clarification of the company's financial position' is attached to the notice of suspension, investors should fear the worst. It usually means that the company has run out of cash and can't persuade its bankers to put up any more.

Usually, but mercifully not always. Sometimes it really does mean that the financial position is being sorted out.

## Companies delisting

Companies are also more inclined to quit AIM than they are to leave the main market. Examples are:

- **Merchant Securities**, a financial services company specialising in stockbroking, wealth management and coporate finance advice. The shares were suspended in December 2011 after a private equity firm took a majority stake and were delisted two months later.

- **Jacques Vert,** the clothes retailer. After years of struggling to cope in the highly competitive High Street, the company succumbed readily to a takeover at the end of 2011.

- **Artisan,** a house builder and property investor. Prolonged difficult market conditions after the credit crunch brought falling turnover and pre-tax losses. Talks with banks on refinancing dragged on for months until the company decided in late 2011 that it could no longer afford the luxury of an AIM quotation and the shares were removed in February 2012

# Chapter 8
## How Shares Are Traded

When share trading started in the coffee houses of London in the 17th century investors would have met face to face to make deals. However, the system became increasingly impractical as the number of investors and companies grew. This was the beginning of stock exchanges, which grew up around the country. It was found more efficient for all interested investors to meet in one designated exchange where the best prices could be found in an ordered market.

In the past, investors placed their buy orders with a stockbroker, who passed on the requests to a jobber, who carried out the actual trade on the trading room floor by finding another jobber trying to sell a similar amount of the same shares at roughly the same price at pretty much the same time.

The jobbers would ensure the smooth functioning of the market by always offering to buy or sell shares – at a price. Although this system worked reasonably well for a couple of centuries, it was an expensive, time consuming and not altogether satisfactory way of doing business in the modern era, though you had probably guessed that already.

Towards the end of the 20th century, advances in technology and finance sparked a revolution in how shares were traded. Or perhaps one should say evolution, for the LSE very sensibly developed improvements in trading at a steady rather than spectacular pace, so the system never broke down and was constantly getting better.

Trading now is carried out on computer screens among stockbrokers and other serious traders willing to pay for the privilege of access to the London Stock Exchange's trading system. Trading is instantaneous and the jobbers have been consigned to history.

## Different forms of trading

Because companies of all sorts and sizes seek to have their shares quoted on the stock market, the London Stock Exchange has created different trading platforms (different ways in which buy and sell orders are matched up).

These are based on how liquid the shares are. Liquidity refers to how active trading in a particular share is. The most liquid shares, such as those in HSBC, BP or Vodafone, see a trade go through every few seconds throughout the day. Illiquid shares may see a whole day go by without a single deal being struck.

Shares in smaller companies may be illiquid, in other words there are fewer buyers and sellers around, perhaps because there are fewer shares in issue, or the company is little known and does not attract the interest of investors, or perhaps large blocks of shares are in the hands of a few major investors who rarely sell.

While AIM stocks tend on the whole to be smaller and less liquid than those on the main board, we are seeing increasingly that companies at the top end of AIM are larger and their shares are more liquid than fledgling stocks with a full listing.

## Market makers

Initially after Big Bang, all shares had market makers. These were stockbrokers willing to guarantee to buy or sell shares in particular companies – they were never expected to cover all companies on the stock exchange as that would have tied up too much capital.

They posted their buy and sell prices on the stock exchange's electronic system and kept some shares of each company on their books to fulfil any buy orders they received. Prices would rise and fall according to demand from buyers and sellers as market makers attempted to balance their books, buying and selling roughly equal numbers of shares in each company each day.

Market makers, like jobbers, have been overtaken by history as the LSE improved its trading system; although they still create a market in the most illiquid stocks, ensuring that there is always a buyer and a seller available.

## SETS

This is the LSE's flagship electronic order book: the Stock Exchange Electronic Trading System. Companies have been added to it a few at a time, starting with the largest and most liquid, so that it now accounts for all the 350 largest companies, plus all except the very smallest ones, with a full listing.

The larger, more liquid stocks with an AIM quotation are also now traded on SETS.

A full list of companies traded on SETS can be found at:

**www.londonstockexchange.com/products-and-services/sets/list-sets.xls**

If you want to buy, your broker will post your bid price and the number of shares you are looking for onto the trading system from its office computer. If you want to sell, your offer price and number of shares for sale are similarly posted.

When a buyer and a seller post the same price, the two are automatically matched up. If, say, the buyer wants 2,000 shares and the seller is offering 3,000 shares, the deal is struck for 2,000 shares (the lower figure) and a sale offer for 1,000 shares remains on the computer system.

Anyone with access to the trading system – and even a private investor can see the prices displayed on several financial websites, though you may have to pay a subscription fee – is able to see not only the best buying and selling prices available but also how many buy or sell orders have been posted and at what prices.

A clear picture can thus be gained of whether one side outnumbers the other and the sort of levels at which buyers would start to bail out if the share price rises, or where supporters would pile in if the price falls.

Figure 1: SETS trading screen

| ASTRAZENECA ORD SHS $0.25 (SET1\FE10) | | | | | Latest Trades | | |
|---|---|---|---|---|---|---|---|
| **Mid:** 3,268 +19 (+0.58%) | | | | | 14:32:40 | 3267.00 | 20 |
| | | | | | 14:32:21 | 3267.92 | 52,150 |
| NMS: 100,000 Close: 3,249 Uncr: 3,248 | | | | | 14:32:26 | 3269.00 | 162 |
| Spread: 0.06% Open: 3,248 VWAP: 3,255.37 | | | | | 14:32:24 | 3268.00 | 838 |
| Trd Hi: 3,280 Total Vol: 3,207,172 | | | | | 14:32:24 | 3269.00 | 3,000 |
| Trd Lo: 3,226 SETS Vol: 2,201,981 | | | | | 14:32:24 | 3269.00 | 1,840 |
| Status: OBT - Order Book Trading | | | | | 14:32:24 | 3268.00 | 1,160 |
| 3 8,777 3,267 3,269 5,938 2 | | | | | 14:32:23 | 3268.00 | 240 |
| | | | | | 14:32:23 | 3268.00 | 2,760 |
| | | | | | 14:32:20 | 3268.00 | 11 |
| BUY ORDERS Filter(%): | | SELL ORDERS Filter(%): | | | 14:32:20 | 3268.00 | 329 |
| | | | | | 14:32:14 | 3268.00 | 200 |
| 14:30 | 5,114 | 3,267 | 3,269 | 4,238 | 14:32 | 3268.00 | 71 |
| 14:31 | 2,957 | 3,267 | 3,269 | 1,700 | 14:32:14 | 3268.00 | 2,290 |
| 14:32 | 706 | 3,266 | 3,271 | 1,900 | 14:31:56 | 3268.00 | 696 |
| 14:32 | 725 | 3,266 | 3,272 | 2,000 | 14:31:53 | 3268.00 | 1,914 |
| 14:32 | 600 | 3,266 | 3,272 | 5,000 | 14:31:52 | 3268.00 | 286 |
| 14:31 | 2,443 | 3,265 | 3,272 | 700 | 14:31:52 | 3268.00 | 600 |
| 14:32 | 3,750 | 3,265 | 3,273 | 19,798 | 14:31:52 | 3268.00 | 14 |
| 14:32 | 3,000 | 3,265 | 3,273 | 700 | 14:31:51 | 3268.00 | 2,186 |
| 14:32 | 100 | 3,265 | 3,274 | 3,750 | 14:31:01 | 3268.00 | 1,714 |
| 14:32 | 100 | 3,264 | 3,274 | 5,000 | 14:31:00 | 3268.00 | 908 |
| 14:32 | 2,719 | 3,264 | 3,275 | 9,747 | 14:31:00 | 3268.00 | 200 |
| 14:32 | 5,000 | 3,262 | 3,275 | 1,000 | | | 500 |
| 14:32 | 1,000 | 3,261 | 3,276 | 3,000 | | | |
| 14:17 | 5,000 | 3,260 | 3,277 | 3,800 | | | |
| 14:28 | 3,000 | 3,260 | 3,279 | 500 | | | |
| 14:32 | 500 | 3,254 | 3,290 | 7,000 | | | |

(yellow strip)

Here is a typical Level 2 screen showing pharmaceuticals giant AstraZenica as it appeared on the website MoneyAM (which provides free access to Level 2 – you just have to register with the site).

At the top we see that the latest mid price (half way between the buying and selling prices) is 3,268p, which is 19p or 0.58% higher than the previous closing price of 3,249p. We can see that the shares opened at 3,248p and have traded as high as 3,280p and as low as 3,226p during the latest trading session.

The yellow horizontal band (appropriately called the "yellow strip") tells us that three bidders are offering to buy a total of 8,777 shares at 3,267p (i.e. if you want to sell shares, this is the current highest selling price available), and two sellers are offering to sell a total of 5,938 shares at 3,269p (i.e. if you are a buyer, this is the lowest buying price available).

In the bottom left hand section we can see all the prevailing buy and sell orders, with the best buy and sell orders at the top; colour bands indicate orders at the same price. A time stamp also indicates the time at which they were placed.

On the far right we see the latest trades to go though, with the time that each bargain was struck, the price and the number of shares traded.

## The spread

Note that there will always be a gap between the highest buying price on offer and the lowest selling price. This is known as the spread.

With reference to the previous screenshot for AstraZeneca, the spread between the best buying and selling price at this precise moment is 2p and the mid price is 3,268p.

That looks to be an unusually wide spread for such a large company – we would normally expect a gap of no more than 1p - but we should remember that it is in fact quite tiny when you consider that Astra shares cost more than £30 each.

The moment a seller matches the highest buying price, or a buyer agrees to pay the lowest selling price, a deal is done instantaneously. The second best price immediately replaces the order that was fulfilled as being the best on offer and the gap is re-established.

Highly liquid stocks will tend to have a spread of 0.5p or even 0.25p. There will always be new buyers and new sellers piling in to close the gap between best prices on offer. The less liquid the stock is, the wider the spread is likely to be.

When you read a share price in a newspaper you will see the 'middle price' which is half way between the lowest selling and highest buying prices on offer.

## SETSqx

SETSqx (Stock Exchange Electronic Trading Service – quotes and crosses) is an electronic trading service for securities that are less liquid than those traded on SETS. In October 2007 it replaced various other trading platforms that had been established after Big Bang to create markets in less liquid shares.

A full list of all companies traded on SETSqx can be found at:

**http://www.londonstockexchange.com/products-and-services/tradin g-services/setsqx/ccp-securities.xls**

A detailed explanation of how the system works can be found at:

**http://www.londonstockexchange.com/products-and-services/tradin g-services/setsqx/sets-brochure.pdf**

This system is slightly more complicated than SETS as it involves market makers and there are four auctions each day at which market makers can square up their books. There is no need to understand fully the intricacies of SETSqx as you can place orders with your broker in exactly the same way as for SETS stocks.

However, you should be aware that the spread between the buying and selling price is likely to be wider for SETSqx stocks.

## SEAQ

This is the land where market makers still roam free, the non-electronic alternative to SETS and SETSqx.

Only illiquid AIM stocks are traded on the Stock Exchange Alternative Quotation (SEAQ) system. They can not be traded on SETS because there would be times when no buy or sell offers were posted and trading would grind to a halt.

Instead, at least two market makers guarantee to post buy and se prices throughout stock exchange trading hours. Spreads on SEAQ stocks will be wider than for SETSqx, with 2p or more the norm. It means that if you buy any of these stocks the share prices have to rise further to put you into profit.

A full list of shares traded on SEAQ can be found at:

**http://www.londonstockexchange.com/products-and-services/tradi ng-services/seaq/list-seaq.xls**

## International Order Book

Since the turn of the Millennium the London Stock Exchange has been gradually developing an electronic trading platform for companies quoted on overseas stock exchanges. This has, sensibly, been expanded gradually and it covers about 50 countries, including Central and Eastern Europe, Asia and the Middle East.

The market operates in the same way as SETS and is highly liquid.

It is sensible for beginners to learn to trade and invest in UK stocks first but it is worth bearing in mind that opportunities to invest in foreign companies are opening up.

## Share certificates and CREST

Shareholders have traditionally held pieces of paper called share certificates that record the name of the company whose shares were bought and the number of shares held. Under this arrangement you hand your share certificate back to the broker so that it can be cancelled and a new certificate is issued to the person buying the shares from you.

But this is a cumbersome system. It can take several days for the paperwork to be done and the certificate to be delivered to the new shareholder. Certificates may get lost and without them you cannot prove you own the shares. Replacement certificates can be issued but

the cost of producing them. In short, the system is
…-consuming and expensive.

…matters, the London Stock Exchange has set up an
…ettlement service, called CREST, so that share sales and
purch… can be recorded more easily and more quickly. Investors who fear the electronic world of the 21$^{st}$ century can be assured that this system does work. It was heavily tested over many months before it was launched and share registers were added one or two at a time, starting with the largest companies, so the system was never overloaded.

Shares held in the CREST system are referred to as being in dematerialised or electronic form. That just means they are not printed on paper.

One drawback of CREST is that shares are normally held by your stockbroker in a nominee account, that is an account in the broker's name. The broker has already paid for the right to make transactions through CREST and can easily set up a nominee account for all your transactions, which are kept separate from the broker's other clients.

Unfortunately that means you lose your rights as a shareholder, as the shares will be recorded on the share register in the broker's name, not yours.

You can ask the broker to register shares cleared through CREST in your own name in order to retain your rights to have accounts posted to your home address and to vote at shareholder meetings, but you will have to pay a fee for the privilege. Charges vary so ask your broker how much it will cost.

This option may not be available if you trade through an online broker, where keeping costs to a minimum is paramount. Check with the broker if this is the case.

Whichever system you use for buying and selling shares, any deal you make takes place immediately, irrespective of how long the deal takes to be processed.

# Chapter 9
## Stock Market Indices

It is quite easy to watch the progress of one or two shares day by day but you cannot possibly spot all the movements of all the shares on the London Stock Exchange.

It can, though, be useful to keep track of how the market generally is faring, so you can tell whether your shares are doing better than average or you can watch for warning signs that the market is weak. So a series of stock market indices has been devised which can tell you how the whole market or various parts of it have moved overall during the day.

Each index is calculated as a figure and the size of the change in that figure reflects the scale of the movement of the market as a whole.

On any trading day, some shares rise, others fall and some stand still. Stock market indices average out the changes to give a representative overall picture. Changes are calculated moment by moment, each change in any share price being reflected automatically.

These changes can be recorded on a chart, just as movements of an individual share price are.

Some indices cover companies of a specific size, such as the largest, the medium sized ones or just the tiniest. Others comprise specific sectors, that is all the companies in a particular line of businesses. For example, there are separate indices covering oil and gas, industrials, telecoms and utilities.

Then there are indices for sub-sectors. For instance, as well as an index covering all financial companies there is an index comprising banks, one for life insurance and another for general insurers.

## Meet the Footsie family

While the FTSE 100 index, covering the biggest companies listed on the London Stock Exchange, is the Daddy of them all, there's a whole range of little 'footsies' dancing around to help you to see in which direction the stock market is really running.

FTSE stands for Financial Times Stock Exchange – the operation used to be a joint venture between the *Financial Times* and the London Stock Exchange, but in 2011 the FT sold its share to the LSE.

A FTSE committee decide which companies go into which index. They meet every three months, early in March, June, September and December, always on a Wednesday.

Which companies go into which index will depend on share prices at the close of trading on the previous evening. Any agreed changes will take effect over the weekend that falls 10 days later, so some companies will end the week in one index and start the next week, somewhere round about the 20th day of the month, with a new status.

### FTSE 100

The FTSE 100, the one usually referred to affectionately as the Footsie, is intended to cover the 100 companies with the largest stock market capitalisations (usually abbreviated to market cap). The capitalisation of a company is the value that the stock market puts on the entire company and is calculated by multiplying the share price by the number of shares that have been issued.

The committee does have some leeway is deciding membership of the FTSE 100, otherwise the index would have companies bobbing in and out every quarter.

The top 90 companies must be included. Any company ranked lower than 110 must be excluded. The committee decides which of the 20 companies in between are in and which are out.

The main consideration is stability. Companies already in the top flight will normally be retained even if they slip just outside the top 100 on the day that the axe happens to fall. A company that looks as if it is here to stay will take precedence over one that could be a flash in the pan.

Chart 3: FTSE 100 Index

We can see how events affected the index over a 10-year period. After the peak at just short of 7,000 points in 2000, the index retreated as the tech bubble burst and investors realised that most tech stocks were grossly overvalued, with some not even viable.

As so often happens, the sell-off went too far, just as the earlier boom had done, and investors drove the market back almost to its previous high. Then came the sub-prime scandal, a global economic downturn and the credit crunch in the West and the index fell back rapidly.

The recovery this time was less dramatic, as worries persisted over the crisis in the Eurozone, with Greece, Ireland, Spain, Portugal and Italy struggling to cope with sovereign debt, and economic growth failed to take off in the US and Europe, including the UK.

## FTSE 250

Immediately below the FTSE 100 is the FTSE 250, which covers the next 250 medium sized companies. This is often referred to as the midcap index, the one covering shares with middle-sized capitalisations.

Into this index go all those shares that narrowly missed the FTSE 100 and, again, the committee has discretion over which of the borderline cases are included at the bottom end. Again, we can see how the midcaps moved over 10 years in the following chart..

Chart 4: FTSE 250 Index

At first sight the two charts seem to follow similar patterns, although one or two differences are readily apparent. Both indices hit the bottom on the same day in March 2003, although the FTSE 100 index fell more sharply in the final phase of the bear market.

We can see that the two subsequent peaks in the FTSE 250 were almost equal while the FTSE 100 recovery in 2010-11 ran out of steam well short of its all-time high in 2007.

However, comparing the above chart of the FTSE 250 Index with that of the FTSE 100 Index, it is not easy to spot which index has been the stronger performer. This can be seen better in the following chart, in which the two indices are re-based to the same starting point.

Chart 5: FTSE 100 Index v FTSE 250 Index

Two points emerge:

1. The FTSE 250 is far more volatile than the FTSE 100.
2. The FTSE 250 is likely to turn the corner after reaching a peak or trough earlier than the FTSE 100.

The overall picture is that it was possible to make more trading profits in midcap stocks, reflecting the higher degree of risk and the emergence of new potential high fliers that had previously been unnoticed and undervalued.

One other reason for the apparently sluggish performance of the FTSE 100 index is that its component companies were more likely to pay steady dividends and the investment rewards came in income rather than share price gains.

## FTSE 350

These two indexes are combined in the FTSE 350 index comprising the 350 largest companies. This is an often ignored member of the family. After all, it tells you little that you can't see separately in the 100 and 250 versions.

The FTSE 100, 250 and 350 all contain precisely the number of companies that are in their names but the other indexes that are worth looking at are elastic. They grow or shrink according to the number of companies that happen to be kicking around.

## FTSE Small Cap index and FTSE Fledgling index

The FTSE Small Cap index covers the smaller (but not quite the smallest) companies with a stock market listing. The smallest of all go into the FTSE Fledgling index.

## FTSE All-Share

Just to show that we have one big happy Footsie family, all the companies included in the various indices are lumped together in the

FTSE All-Share index, which gives us an overall view of the main stock market board.

There are also FTSE indices for the different sectors such as banking, construction, mining and leisure. These enable investors to gauge how well a particular company is faring compared with its peers, as its rivals are referred to.

The Footsie family has a cousin, the AIM index, which, as its name implies, comprises the stocks quoted on the Alternative Investment Market.

There is an AIM 100 index comprising the 100 largest AIM stocks, including foreign companies, and an AIM UK 50 index comprising the 50 largest UK stocks on AIM.

## Weightings

Every day some shares go up, some go down and some are unchanged. That happens even when the stock market as a whole is moving strongly in one direction or another. In addition, some shares may move heavily on a particular day while others change just one or two pence.

Each index must therefore calculate the average overall movement of the constituent companies. Companies are weighted according to their stock market capitalisations so share price movements of larger companies have a greater impact than those of smaller companies.

This prevents a sharp change in the share price of a small company having a disproportionate effect on an index, especially the All-Share index.

The following table is taken from the FTSE website (**www.ftse.com**); it shows the weightings of the ten largest stocks in June 2011. Note that the companies, and certainly their weightings, can change over time.

You can ignore the ICB Code – this is a unique code for each company allotted jointly by the FTSE and the Dow Jones Index.

**Table 8: FTSE weightings for top 10 constituents**

| Constituent | ICB Code | ICB Sector | Net Mkt Cap (GBPm) | Weight (%) FTSE 100 Index Index | Weight (%) FTSE All-Share Index |
|---|---|---|---|---|---|
| HSBC Hldgs | 8350 | Banks | 110,182 | 7.11 | 6.00 |
| BP | 0530 | Oil & Gas Producers | 86,422 | 5.58 | 4.71 |
| Vodafone Group | 6570 | Mobile Telecommunications | 84,755 | 5.47 | 4.62 |
| Royal Dutch Shell A | 0530 | Oil & Gas Producers | 79,739 | 5.15 | 4.34 |
| GlaxoSmithKline | 4570 | Pharmaceuticals & Biotechnology | 69,197 | 4.47 | 3.77 |
| Rio Tinto | 1770 | Mining | 67,388 | 4.35 | 3.67 |
| Royal Dutch Shell B | 0530 | Oil & Gas Producers | 60,423 | 3.90 | 3.29 |
| British American Tobacco | 3780 | Tobacco | 54,525 | 3.52 | 2.97 |
| BHP Billiton | 1770 | Mining | 52,432 | 3.39 | 2.86 |
| BG Group | 0530 | Oil & Gas Producers | 47,641 | 3.08 | 2.59 |
| Totals | | | 712,703 | 46.02 | 38.82 |

Source: : FTSE Group, data as at 30 Jun, 2011

Before the credit crunch the top ten was dominated by banks. Now only one remains, admittedly in top spot. Banks were replaced by Oil & Gas as the most prominent sector.

# SECTION C
## Companies

# Chapter 10
## Company Focus

## What does the company do?

### Companies and groups

Just as stocks and shares have become synonymous, so too the terms company and group have become interchangeable.

Strictly speaking, a company is one single business entity while a group is a group of companies all under the same ownership.

In a group, there will be a parent company that owns the various parts of the empire, which are the subsidiary companies kept separate for administrative convenience because they are into different lines of business or they operate in different countries.

Sometimes the parent company produces goods and services as well. In some cases the parent company does little itself and simply exists as the umbrella under which the subsidiaries operate. In that case the parent is a holding company and the subsidiaries are operating companies.

A company concentrating on just one line of products or services may not need to split itself into different units but if it does do so it will form divisions with the head of each division reporting to the one chief executive.

Dividing groups or companies in this way means it is easier to see which part of the operations are doing well and to spot problems as they arise.

## What a company does

You need to have a good idea of what a company actually does before you invest in it. You wouldn't buy a tin off the supermarket shelf without knowing what was inside it, would you?

Some companies compete head on with others producing the same range of products or services; others try to find a niche market, concentrating on just one product where they are the biggest or only player.

Some companies believe in having a wide spread of products so that if demand falls off for one they have other lines to fall back on; while some specialise so they know their business inside out (a tactic referred to as sticking to their knitting).

Some concentrate on the UK, or even just one region; others want to go out and conquer the world.

# Assessing a company

## How to assess a company

Having established what the company does, you should consider whether it is expanding. Are sales rising or falling? While turnover is less important than profits, a company that is selling less and less is not going to survive long unless it can stabilise its income.

Is the company a heavy user of energy or fuel? It is likely to be suffering from higher costs unless it is able to pass those costs on in increased prices to its own customers.

Another important consideration is the extent to which the company has fixed costs such as offices and factory production lines. If sales go up and costs remain fairly static then profits will automatically rise. However, if sales fall and costs cannot be cut, the effect on profits can be pretty dramatic.

## The importance of management

No one tactic guarantees success or is doomed to failure. You are looking for companies that demonstrate that they know what they are doing, whatever it is. Good management counts for a great deal.

So you want to know if top executives have changed recently. A poorly performing company can be turned round by new management who have fresh ideas and are determined to prove a point. A great company can tail off when the driving forces retire.

Really well-run companies plan for the succession. They avoid having the two top men, the chairman and the chief executive, retire at the same time. They set the search for a successor rolling in good time. Finding a high quality candidate for a top job can take months of searching by expensive recruitment firms popularly known as headhunters.

So management matters. But so does what the company does. Some sectors such as construction and housebuilding have been expanding for years despite interest rate rises while shops have struggled to cope with intense competition in the high street and with the incursions of online retailers.

## Where to find information on a company

Ascertaining this information may seem daunting but you should try to build up as accurate a picture of a prospective investment as you can before committing your cash and it is not as difficult as you think.

Listed companies maintain websites with up-to-date information on what the company does, its financial performance, who the directors are and a host of other facts. From August 2007 AIM companies have been obliged to maintain a website with key information. Get Googling!

The website will also contain press releases and any trading statements the company has issued and copies of the annual report and the most recent company results. These give you a picture of how the directors assess the company's performance over the past year and the outlook for the coming months.

Do read any such pronouncements with a critical eye, though. The directors may be putting the best gloss on a difficult situation. If they have delivered on promises in the past they are more likely to do so in the future. Repeated broken promises are a warning sign and you should be loath to take mere platitudes at face value.

It is true that past performance is no guarantee that there will be more of the same in the future. However, past performance is the most accurate guide you have got.

## Which companies to invest in

Do not invest in companies you do not understand. For example, if a company develops drugs and you cannot grasp the intricacies of Phase I, II and III trials – not many people do – then avoid the sector until you do. If you want to invest in insurance brokers and reinsurance companies, you had better find out what Lloyd's of London is all about.

Nor should you go to the other extreme and invest only in the sector you happen to work in on the grounds that that is all you understand. Portfolios should be balanced with one stock in each of a range of say ten sectors to give you a fair cross section.

If you bought shares in HSBC, Royal Bank of Scotland, Barclays, Lloyds TSB, Northern Rock and HBoS in the early years of the Millennium and nothing else you were up the creek when banking shares went into a dive in 2008. The banks may have been too big for the government to allow them to fail but four of the six in that list were not too big to fail their shareholders.

The notion of investing only in ethical companies has become trendy in recent years. By all means follow your conscience but bear in mind there is hardly any company in existence that you can't find some objection to. Placing any kind of restriction on which shares you buy can limit your opportunity to make money. You can make only ethical investments and succeed; it is just more difficult.

# Chapter 11
## Income Statement (Profit And Loss)

Companies normally publish their accounts twice a year:

1. the ones issued after the end of the half year are called the *interims*, and

2. those issued after the full year are called the *prelims* or *finals*.

A minority of companies, mainly large ones with international operations such as BP and Shell, issue quarterly accounts, in which case there are three interims and one final. For the sake of clarity we will concentrate on the majority of cases where there is just one interim set of results.

Strictly speaking the accounts are issued in the annual report but a full, preliminary version covering the 12 months is issued through the stock exchange so you do not have to wait longer than necessary. Hence the term 'prelims'. Rest assured, these are the real accounts.

You don't have to understand every detail in a company's accounts but you really should not contemplate making an investment without some basic idea of how well the company is doing.

Unfortunately attempts over the years to improve accounting standards have made company accounts more opaque rather than easier to understand so we shall look at the important elements that give you a clear picture of what is going on.

There are two parts to the accounts:

1. **income statement** (formerly called the profit and loss account) which tells you what went on over the past six or 12 months: how much money came in, how much was spent, how much tax is due and what dividend is proposed, and

2. **balance sheet**, which tells you the state of play at the end of the period, effectively how much the business was worth at that moment in time.

In this chapter we will look at the first part, the profit and loss account, which is increasingly being referred to as the income statement. The next chapter will deal with the balance sheet.

## Analysis of a sample company accounts

Let us look at the table provided in the annual results for Morrisons, the supermarket chain. This is nothing like as fearsome as it appears at first sight. Most items in the list you can work out for yourself with a little common sense.

Table 9: sample company annual results

| Morrisons | 2012 | 2011 | Change |
|---|---|---|---|
| Turnover | £17,663m | £16,479m | + 7% |
| Gross profit | £1,217m | £1,148m | + 6% |
| Other operating income | £86m | £80m | + 8% |
| Administrative expenses | (£329m) | (£323m) | + 8% |
| Underlying operating profit | £974m | £905m | + 8% |
| Property transactions | (£1m) | (£1m) | |
| Operating profit | £973m | £904m | + 8% |
| Net finance charges | (£26m) | (£30m) | - 13% |
| Tax | (£257m) | (£242m) | + 6% |
| Profit after tax | £690m | £632m | + 9% |

Let's take it from the top.

## Turnover

Turnover – which is increasingly referred to as *revenue* these days and can also be called *sales* – is the total amount of money that Morrisons received for its products over the 12 months. We can see by looking at the columns that turnover rose compared to the previous year; it is usual for companies to provide the percentage change, which gives investors a ready check on what progress if any has been made.

Naturally we would prefer companies with rising sales. If sales are down we would need a persuasive explanation before considering the company as an acceptable investment.

## Gross profit

This is the amount left after deducting the cost of making those sales. In the case of Morrisons, costs would include goods bought in to sell, warehousing and distribution, staff costs, and possibly rental payments, council tax, insurance and electricity.

Some companies give cost of sales as a separate line between sales and gross profits.

If the company is recording a loss at this stage it has serious problems and you will need a pretty good explanation to even think about buying the shares. A gross loss would mean that it costs more to produce the goods than the price at which they can be sold, hardly an encouraging sign.

## Other operating income

This line will not appear in all statements. It covers any income that comes from sources outside the normal operations of the company, such as renting out premises to another company or from investments.

## Administrative expenses

This figure appears in brackets because it is a negative figure showing money flowing out.

Companies have other expenses that are not directly connected to the product itself. Examples are wages of administrative and marketing staff. These are described in this statement as administrative expenses; in other cases they may be called overheads or central costs.

There are some grey areas as to which category an expense should go into, for example electricity and storage, but don't worry about that as long as the company is using the same definitions each year so you can make fair comparisons. The important thing is to check whether sales are going up faster than costs (good news) or whether costs are going up faster than sales (bad news).

## Underlying operating profit

This item will appear only if there are other factors not directly connected with trading that distort the figures. In this case we see there are property transactions.

## Property transactions

This line indicates that Morrisons spent (the figure is in brackets so shows an outflow) £1 million on property transactions that were not part of its normal business in both years.

## Operating profit or loss

After deducting all expenses from revenue, we arrive at the operating profit or loss. There is good news for Morrisons shareholders, as operating profits are not only higher year on year but the 8% increase is slightly better than the increase in turnover, indicating that the operations have become marginally more profitable.

The operating profit or loss represents the financial performance of the actual business.

## Net finance charges

The company calculates the interest it paid on any money borrowed minus any income it received from cash in hand. This figure is normally an outgoing shown in brackets, as in this case, but if the company has no borrowings and spare cash invested it would be a plus figure.

Morrison has presumably reduced the amount it has borrowed or else negotiated lower rates of interest on its borrowings because the figure has come down.

## Pre-tax profit or loss

Most companies will show a pre-tax profit or loss at this point in the table, a figure that takes into account all the income and spending apart from taxation on profits.

## Tax

Morrison pays tax on its profits like the rest of us. Again this is a negative figure in brackets unless the company receives a tax rebate. The bill has risen 6% from £242 million to £257 million but at least that is less than the increase in profits.

## Profit or loss after tax

That leaves us with the profit or loss after tax, also referred to as the post tax figure. As always, a loss is shown in brackets.

## Earnings per share

All companies are obliged to show earnings per share somewhere within the income statement. This is very important to you. It is calculated by dividing the profits after tax by the number of shares in issue and shows the amount of profit for each share that you hold.

You may find two EPS figures in some accounts, one diluted and one undiluted. The undiluted figure is the real figure; the diluted figure is what EPS would have been if any convertible shares had been converted into ordinary shares or if any outstanding share options had been exercised.

As we noted right at the start of this book, all ordinary shares have an equal stake in the company. When new shares are issued, your holding stays the same but there are now more shares in existence so the company is divided up into more slices. You will hold a fractionally lower percentage of the company. This effect is referred to as dilution.

Similarly if a company decides to use surplus cash to buy back and cancel shares, the number of shares in issue goes down and the cake is cut into fewer slices.

The earnings per share figure is particularly important if the company has made an acquisition that was paid for in shares. Any extra profits from the acquisition as well as those from the existing business now have to be divided up among more shares.

## Dividends

Dividends are paid out of earnings. If a company makes earnings of 10p per share and pays total dividends (the interim plus the final dividend) of 5p then you know there is easily enough cash to pay the dividends.

This calculation is known as dividend cover – a reference to how comfortable you can feel about the dividend. As far as one can set a norm, companies aim to cover the dividend roughly twice, in other words earnings per share are double the total dividend payment. This allows some leeway to maintain the dividend at the same rate next year even if the company does not do quite as well.

It also means that the company has a surplus that can be used as working capital, to expand the business, to buy new machinery, to acquire another company or to repay bank borrowings.

As long as the dividend is covered by earnings at least once, then profits are sufficient to pay the dividend. However, if cover falls below one then the company will have to draw on its reserves to pay part of the dividend. The reserves are the cash that was tucked away from profits in previous years when the dividend was covered more than once.

If the company makes a loss per share, then the entire dividend will have to be paid out of reserves. This is clearly a worrying sign unless there are genuine hopes that the company will return to making a profit soon. Companies cannot go on drawing down reserves indefinitely. Indeed, when the reserves are used up it is illegal to pay a dividend.

These are the main lines that you definitely need to know in reading a profit and loss account but you will see other entries which can vary from company to company.

## Exceptionals and extraordinaries

Particularly contentious in the profit and loss account are exceptional and extraordinary items. Companies will attempt to pick out large one-off items and list them separately on the grounds that they distort the underlying figures. By underlying we mean the normal business profits that allow us to make meaningful comparisons from year to year.

One-off items would include the sale of a property that was no longer needed. Say a company had two factories making the same item. Putting the whole production into one factory might be more efficient and it would then be possible to sell the empty factory and put the proceeds to good use.

That would create an extraordinary profit from the sale of the factory ('extraordinary' because the main activity of the company was not investing in property – and such profit would be unlikely to recur the following year). On the other hand, deciding that assets previously regarded as valuable were after all worthless would create an extraordinary loss.

No-one has come up with a satisfactory definition of what constitutes an extraordinary item and what makes an exceptional item.

One definition is that:

- an *extraordinary* item is an abnormality that arises from events or transactions that fall outside the ordinary activities of the business and are therefore not likely to recur;

- an *exceptional* item is an unusual large item that falls within the normal activities of the company.

You may see in an income statement a reference to 'normalised' profits. This figure strips out all exceptional and extraordinary items to give the underlying profit. It means that you have a more accurate comparison of profits year by year.

If you think that this is all rather imprecise you are in good company. Some analysts argue that there is no such thing as either and that all profits and losses should be lumped together.

Certainly it is true that many so-called extraordinary losses are really normal business costs that would usually have been spread over several years. In any case, as far as the investors are concerned a profit is a profit and a loss is a loss. After all, routine sales made this year might not be repeated in the future. Is a big contract win an extraordinary item? Surely not, but it could seriously affect profits from one year to the next.

---

### Case study: Persimmon

As the housing market began to recover from the 2008 crash, house builders such as Persimmon saw life in an entirely different context.

At the bottom of the market, they had been awash with land bought at high prices in the boom times – typically builders like to own enough land to last for five or six years at current building rates – and they had borrowings run up to pay for the land.

In the aftermath of the credit crunch and the mortgage famine, house builders scrambled to reduce borrowings and in some case to offload surplus land. All this activity caused distortions in the profit figures so it was difficult to judge whether the underlying business was turning the corner.

For the 2011 calendar year Persimmon reported the following profits, plus a comparison with the previous year:

Table 10: profits before and after exceptionals

| Persimmon | 2011 before exceptionals | 2011 Exceptionals | 2011 total | 2010 before exceptionals | 2010 Exceptionals | 2010 total |
|---|---|---|---|---|---|---|
| Gross profit | £223.9m | £13.3m | £236.3m | £194.8m | £80.2m | £275.0m |
| Operating profit | £153.0m | £13.3m | £166.3m | £128.7m | £80.2m | £208.9m |
| Pre-tax profit | £143.7m | £3.5m | £147.2m | £90.9 | £63m | £153.9m |

Source: Company annual results

We can see that at all levels of the business – gross profit (revenue minus cost of sales), operating profit (after including operating expenses such as admin costs) and pre-tax profit (after including finance costs) – total profits are down on the previous year.

However, if we strip out the exceptional items we see that underlying profits were higher at all levels.

The exceptional items are all explained in the notes in Persimmon's annual report if you want to see them, but be warned, they are complicated. They include paying off loan notes early with surplus cash; cancelling hedging contracts associated with these loans; writing down the value of some land bought when prices were high; and upgrading the value of other land.

None of these directly affected how well Persimmon had fared in building and selling houses over the period.

Extraordinary and exceptional items must always be explained in the results statement. Usually there will be a separate column next to the table of results directing your attention to relevant notes right at the end of the statement, way after the balance sheet and any other tables such as cash flow that the company might care to include.

If in doubt, go by the pre-tax profit or loss, bearing in mind any items that may have caused a distortion. A loss, extraordinary or otherwise, means the company is less able to increase its dividend while a whacking great extraordinary gain can bring a special, extra dividend.

What you are looking for is whether the company is on an improving trend. If the profit figures are, on the whole, moving upwards (or the loss downwards) then you will naturally be reassured. Always, though, retain at least a grain of suspicion. If you are doubtful about what a company's profit and loss account is saying, there are plenty more companies about and you can't invest in all of them.

## Cash flow

There may be a line in the accounts showing whether cash has flowed in or out of the company. Cash flow is not the same as profit. For instance, a company may invest heavily in new machinery. This will take cash out of the business in the current year, while depreciation of the asset will be taken out of profits bit by bit over several years.

Cash flow is likely to be more lumpy than profits so don't be too worried if some years cash flows out and other years it flows in. You should only be concerned if cash flows out constantly.

The table below for Greggs, the food retailer, shows that changes in cash flow from its operations can vary considerably from changes in pre-tax profits.

Table 11: sample cash flow

| Greggs | 2007 | 2008 | 2009 | 2010 | 2011 |
|---|---|---|---|---|---|
| Pre-tax profits | £49.47m | £49.47m | £48.78m | £52.52m | £60.05m |
| Cash flow | £74.68m | £59.16m | £87.94m | £77.8m | £88.1m |

Source: Company annual results

Profits stagnated in the first three columns while cash flow sank then bounced back. Profits then rose while cash flow again bounced down and back up.

## EBITDA

You will occasionally see a line in the results showing EBITDA or possibly EBIT. This was a device used in the dotcom boom to make unprofitable companies look profitable, or at least minimise the losses.

EBITDA became highly discredited when loss making dotcom companies ran out of money and crashed but it still persists and you should be extremely suspicious if you see a company pushing the EBITDA figure rather than the pre-tax profit figure. It almost certainly means that the company is making a pre-tax loss.

EBITDA stands for earnings before interest, tax, depreciation and amortisation. It is roughly equivalent to operating profit except that it may be shown as earnings per share rather than a total figure, in other words the profit has been divided by the number of shares in issue.

As you can see, it is calculated before a number of deductions, which is why the figure tends to be flattering and hence beloved by companies losing money. The case for ignoring these deductions varies from weak to non-existent.

Let us take the items one by one as they appear in this ludicrous acronym.

## Interest

Interest we all understand. The company borrows from the bank and it has to pay interest on the debt, as we all do. If a company borrows heavily to finance its operations, then those operations must produce enough income to cover the interest bill, otherwise there's not much point in bothering to get out of bed in the morning.

Now companies can, for a limited period, run up debt without repaying it and even without paying all the interest as it is incurred, just as you can run up bills on your credit card and get away with simply coughing up the minimum amount. This state of affairs can not, however, go on indefinitely.

Interest payments are a genuine part of business expenses and cannot be ignored in calculating profits.

## Depreciation

Taking depreciation out of the equation is slightly, just slightly, more acceptable. Where a company buys capital equipment, say a piece of machinery, it will last for several years. Once it is paid for, there is no need to splash out on a replacement until it wears out.

Nonetheless, it is prudent to write off a percentage of the value of the equipment year by year. This is rather like the value of your car. You pay £20,000 because that is what it is worth new but after just one year it will have lost about a quarter of its value to around £15,000 and after three years it will probably be worth less than half what you paid for it.

Companies therefore depreciate assets to represent dwindling values. Failure to include depreciation in the profit figure would mean taking a great chunk out of profits in a single year when the equipment needed replacing.

Interest and depreciation, therefore, are genuine expenses and should definitely be included when calculating profits.

### Amortisation

Omitting amortisation is more reasonable. Amortisation occurs when a company buys another company. Say the acquisition has assets of £100m but it is a good little earner and it is bought for £120m because of its potential. The extra £20m is referred to as goodwill. This will be written off in the annual results in equal amounts until all the goodwill is accounted for, a process known as amortisation.

This is arguably an accounting technicality rather than a normal business cost.

### Tax

Finally we come to T for tax. This is certainly fair enough. All companies produce figures for pre-tax and post-tax profits. However, we do need to be sure that the company can afford to pay its tax bill at the end of the day and you don't know that from the EBITDA figure.

Therefore be highly suspicious of EBITDA. It does not give a true picture of how the company is doing.

## Seasonal sales

Some companies make most of their money in one particular part of the year or around a specific date. Such companies with seasonal sales and profits will tend to put the worst part of the year into the first half so they can always hold out the hope of better things to come if early sales slump.

Many obvious examples spring to mind.

Despite the popularity of winter sports among those who can keep their balance on the piste, holiday companies sell the overwhelming majority of their deals for the summer season. It is hard to think of a holiday provider that does not make a loss every winter.

The following table shows the difference between first half trading to March 31 and second half trading to September 30 for holiday company Thomas Cook. Figures in brackets are losses.

Table 12: sample seasonal revenue and profits

| Thomas Cook | First half 2010 | Second half 2010 | First half 2011 | Second half 2011 |
|---|---|---|---|---|
| Revenue | £3309m | £5581m | £3431.m | £6318m |
| Operating profit | (£130m) | £490m | (£166m) | £470m |
| Pre-tax profit | (£252m) | £500m | (£269m) | £444m |

Source: company results

Jewellers, on the other hand, make most of their money in December as conscience-stricken husbands attempt to make up for the past year's indiscretions.

Chocolates also sell heavily at Christmas but they have a bonus at Valentine's Day and at Easter. Spring is a time when a young man's fancy turns not only to love … but also to garden centres.

Do not, however, rush out to buy shares in chocolates maker and retailer Thornton's at the beginning of February just because sales are about to take off for a couple of weeks.

The peaks and troughs of the sales seasons are factored in, that is taken into account, when investors assess the shares. They will shoot up or down only if the company subsequently reports a particularly good or poor peak season compared to the same period the previous year.

Companies with seasonal sales need a good supply of cash or available bank loans handy to see them through the thin months so by all means check that sufficient finance is available. By placing their year end just after the busiest period they ensure that debt levels are at their lowest or cash in hand at its highest when the figures are produced.

## Segments

The company may break its turnover and profits down into segments so you have a better idea of seeing which bits are doing well and which are causing problems.

A housebuilder such as Barrett Developments, with sites all over the country, may split its report into regions. This is important if, for instance, house prices in the south east are taking off while those in Yorkshire are marking time. You can see whether the company is more heavily committed to the thriving parts of the country or the less well favoured.

An international company such as Imperial Tobacco will tell you how its sales are going in various parts of the world. This can be important because the West has been running a long campaign to alert smokers to health risks while Third World countries are a growing market. Shareholders want to know if sales are being pushed in the fastest expanding market.

Results for insurer Legal & General included the following table of operating profits:

Table 13: sample profits by geographic segment

| Legal & General | 2010 | 2011 |
|---|---|---|
| USA | £85m | £104m |
| Europe (Netherlands and France) | £26m | £41m |
| Egypt, the Gulf and India | (£9m) | (£8m) |

Source: company results

We can see that profits in the US and Europe were boosted significantly but that losses elsewhere overseas had been trimmed only slightly.

There is no rule that says how companies should divide up their regions – indeed there is no obligation to divide the results up at all.

Much will depend on how widely the company is committed geographically.

Wolseley, the building products supplier, divides in two between Europe and North America. Others may split Europe into north and south or east and west. Some companies with small operations in Africa may have an EMEA region – Europe, the Middle East and Africa. Sometimes Asia Pacific lumps the Far East and Australia/New Zealand together.

An alternative to dividing into geographic areas is to split the business into products or services.

For example, John Menzies, better known as a distributor of newspapers and magazines to newsagents and supermarkets around the UK, has branched out into the somewhat unrelated world of ground handling services at airports.

Don't laugh... news distribution is shrinking along with newspaper circulations while moving air passengers and cargo is rapidly becoming the larger part of the business. Splitting the results into these two segments gives a clearer picture of the group as we see in this table:

Table 14: Menzies turnover and profit by sector

| Menzies | 2010 | 2011 |
|---|---|---|
| Aviation turnover | £626.0m | £676.8m |
| Aviation profit | £24.6m | £32.3m |
| Distribution turnover | £1,338.2m | £1,337.0m |
| Distribution profit | £28.8m | £28.8m |

We can see that the larger distribution subsidiary is merely holding its own while the smaller aviation subsidiary is increasing its turnover and profits.

Don't worry too much about how a company segmentalises. In the end it is the total for the company that matters. Breaking down the figures is just an extra help for you in analysing and assessing the company as a potential investment.

## Comparing like with like

It is important in judging whether a company's performance is improving to know that the latest figures are genuinely comparable with the previous year. Fortunately companies go to much greater pains these days to ensure that they are, even producing a second set of figures to eliminate distortions.

Companies may produce accounts for continuing businesses which strip out the contributions from operations that have been sold during the year.

Retailers in particular will produce figures for total sales and also for like-for-like sales. Total sales will include sales made at stores opened in the course of the year; like-for-likes tell you what happened at stores that traded throughout the past two financial years to give a fair comparison.

The like-for-like figure gives you a genuine indication of whether sales are improving or if they are simply being boosted by the company opening new stores.

## The audit

It is not necessary to have interim accounts audited but full-year results must be checked by an independent firm of auditors which will normally sign the accounts as a going concern. In essence that means the auditor is satisfied that the company is not about to go bust.

If the auditor has any reservations it will 'qualify' the accounts. This is very, very unusual but can happen if the auditors are not satisfied that the company has enough cash to keep going, or the company and auditors disagree over the way figures should be presented.

There are three reasons why auditors may qualify a company's accounts:

1.  They are unable to check some information.

2.  They disagree with the way that an item has been treated in the accounts.

3.  They feel that the accounts do not give a true and fair view of the company's financial position.

One reason why accounts are very rarely qualified is that the company will usually back down and comply with the auditor's wishes rather than suffer the ignominy of an accusing finger.

# Chapter 12
## Balance Sheet

The balance sheet is an assessment of the assets and liabilities of the company at the moment the financial year ends.

- *Assets* are the things of value that the company owns including cash, property and machinery, while

- *liabilities* are what the company owes, such as bills from suppliers and bank loans.

Also note that, as elsewhere, assets are shown as positive figures on the balance sheet while liabilities are shown in brackets.

The balance sheet will show the figures for the latest year end in one column and those for the previous year end in a separate column so you can see what changes in assets and liabilities have been incurred over the financial year.

As with the profit and loss account, items on the balance sheet can vary from company to company and you do not need to understand every single line comprehensively but it is useful to get the general picture so that you can assess the overall health of the company and whether it is moving in the right direction.

The annual results and the annual report will usually have notes at the end explaining the various items in the balance sheet.

Lets us again use the Morrisons results statement to show a typical balance sheet. I have condensed the table to show just the main lines.

Table 15: Morrisons balance sheet

| Morrisons | 2011 | 2012 |
|---|---|---|
| Non-current assets | £8,011m | £8,537m |
| Current assets | £1,138m | £1,322m |
| Current liabilities | £2,086m | £2,303m |
| Non-current liabilities | £1,643m | £2,159m |
| Net assets | £5,420m | £5,397m |

Source: company results

### Fixed (or non-current) assets

The first line on the balance sheet will normally be fixed assets. These are items such as machinery that are used by the business. They are fixed in the sense that they do not vary from day to day in the way that cash in hand or debts do. They are calculated on the basis of what they cost in the first place minus an amount written off the value to cover depreciation or, in the case of property, they are revalued by an independent surveyor at set periods.

This figure may be subdivided into:

- tangible assets, which are things you can see and touch such as equipment and property, and
- intangibles such as goodwill that is a vaguer valuation.

### Current assets

Then come current assets. These may be subdivided into cash at bank and debts that are owed to the company and are due to be paid within 12 months. In other words, these are assets that the company could reasonably hope to lay its hands on fairly quickly.

### Current liabilities

After that we have current liabilities, the amounts that the company is due to pay to people such as its suppliers within the next 12 months.

You deduct current liabilities from current assets. If the figure is a positive one, that figure is called net current assets; if you end up with a negative figure the company has net current liabilities.

The point of this little sum is to see whether the company faces a potential outflow of funds over the next 12 months or whether it has a buffer.

### Non-current liabilities

Apart from current liabilities there may be long term liabilities such as a loan that is not due to be repaid within 12 months. As an alternative to issuing shares, companies may raise money through bonds, which are loans raised from investors rather than banks. They are often referred to as loan stock.

### Net assets

When you deduct total liabilities from total assets you end up with net assets, which again is usually a positive figure but in the case of a company in financial difficulties could be a negative figure (that is, the liabilities exceed the assets) and this will be shown in brackets.

We mentioned that balance sheets can vary according to what line of business the company is in. For example, a bank's balance sheet is likely to contain several more lines covering items such as customers' deposits, financial derivatives and the like. The important lines remain, however, total assets, total liabilities and net assets.

Finally we come to capital and reserves.

### Capital reserves

First we have the called up share capital, which is the number of shares that have been issued multiplied by the nominal value of the shares. So if a company issues 100m shares with a nominal value of 50p each then the called up share capital will be £50m.

As I will explain in the chapter on rights issues and share placings, shares may be issued for more than their face value. The extra amount goes into what is called the share premium account, which is usually shown on the balance sheet.

The balance sheet will also show reserves. These are profits built up over the years and may include property revaluations. It is from these reserves that dividends are paid.

Where a company has made more losses than profits over the years there will be a retained loss, which is the accumulated deficit. A company with a retained loss cannot legally pay a dividend until that loss is wiped out. This stops companies from paying dividends with money they do not have.

# Chapter 13
## Potential Nasties

There are danger signs to watch for in trading statements which may be issued separately or alongside a company's results.

If you are superstitious and believe that bad news always comes in threes then you will feel at home with profit warnings. When things go wrong, it is rare for them to be sorted out in one go. Three profit warnings is the norm, though there can be more.

Note that directors can be as reluctant as investors to face up to the fact that they got it wrong. Being human, they do not go out of their way to highlight the problems. Events at The Game Group, Europe's biggest computer games retailer, provide a classic case.

### Case study: Game Group

Warning signs emerged in April 2011 when disappointing results for the year to 31 January were released. The key figures were:

Table 16: Game Group results

| Game Group | 2010 | 2011 |
|---|---|---|
| Turnover | £1,772.4m | £1,625.0m |
| Gross profit margin | 27.8% | 26.3% |
| Operating profit | £94.8m | £43.2m |
| Pre-tax profit | £84.2m | £23.1m |

Source: company results

Turnover and profit margins were lower; operating profit was cut in half; pre-tax profits were less than a third of the previous year. Yet the dividend was maintained at its previous level and no mention of the profits fall was made in the financial highlights!

Two months later and Game chief executive Ian Shepherd was still putting a gloss on the looming disaster. An interim management statement admitted that the video games market had been 'more challenging' than expected but he claimed to be seeing early results from his 'strategic initiatives' and he reckoned that the pipeline of new hardware and software was encouraging.

This optimism hardly did justice to the situation. Further down the statement came the admission that group sales in Game's financial year so far were down 11.3%. The computer games market as a whole fared even worse with revenue down 12.8% but when your own sales are down so heavily it is little consolation that rivals are faring even worse. With the market shrinking there was little scope for increasing sales.

By the end of September there was still no sign of that pipeline of new products racing to the rescue but once again Shepherd's statement concentrated on assurances that Game was gaining market share. By now, though, there was no denying that trading conditions 'will remain tough for the rest of the year'.

Game reported a first half loss to the end of July, not in itself a surprise as Game, like many retailers, depended heavily on Christmas sales. However, losses had more than doubled and it was clear that there would be little pick-up in the key festive period despite assurances of a 'high quality software line-up'.

Even so, Game decided to maintain the interim dividend rather than conserve cash.

Christmas was a disaster with sales down a whopping 14.7%, even worse than for the earlier, less important, part of the year.

Heavy promotional activity over Christmas hit profit margins at a time when Game should have been raking in the money.

It took press speculation in February 2012 to force Game to admit that it was 'in ongoing dialogue' with its lenders over revising the terms of its borrowing facilities. Roughly translated, that meant that the banks had to pump in £60m to save Game from immediate collapse.

More press reports brought a further admission that Game was in talks with suppliers, some of whom were refusing to let Game have any new products and its was 'uncertain whether any of the solutions being explored by the board will be successful or will result in any value being attributed to the shares of the company'.

Finally Game shares were suspended 'pending clarification of the company's financial position'. This is a phrase that you should fear, as it usually means the company is bust. Game admitted that the shares were probably worthless, which proved to be true as the group soon went into administration.

Chart 6: Game Group

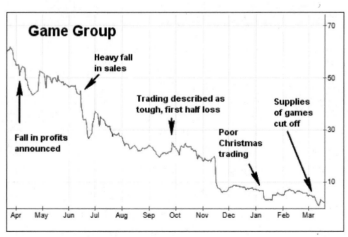

The share chart shows that alert investors started to worry about how hard consumer spending would be squeezed and the impact on computer games sales as soon as the credit crunch broke. By the time Game was saying that its shares might be worthless they were down to around 2p.

## Banking covenants

When companies borrow money from the banks they give promises known as covenants. These will be along the lines of profits being sufficient to cover interest payments and assets being worth more than the loans secured against them.

You may have covenants on your house such as not being allowed to annoy the neighbours or park a caravan on the front lawn. The big difference is that while there is usually no-one to enforce housing covenants, the banks will certainly be keeping an eye on the ones that they impose.

Nor does a company find it any easier to wriggle out of its commitments than you do when you stray over your credit limit. Breaching banking covenants is bad news.

If the indiscretion is a minor one, or merely a technicality, the bank may decide to overlook it, especially if the company has kept the bank fully informed ahead of the actual breach.

At the other end of the scale, the bank may call in the loan and force the company into receivership. It will take such drastic action only in extreme cases. Banks, as you know, prefer to get their money back if they possibly can – and more besides.

So when a company goes along cap in hand the bank demands lengthy talks, for which it charges, and imposes higher interest rates. Thus the struggling company now finds it even harder to meet the bank's requirements.

It can take years of sound trading, and more expensive chats with the bank manager, to get out of this bind.

## Case study: Premier Foods

Britain's biggest food manufacturer, with some of the country's best known brands including Hovis, Mr Kipling and Oxo, was seriously squeezed between rising costs of raw materials, energy and wages on the one hand and supermarkets striving to drive down prices on the other.

Matters came to a head in autumn 2011 when Premier fell out with its largest customer, Tesco, and there were serious doubts as to whether it could continue to cope with debts owed to a syndicate of 28 lenders led by Royal Bank of Scotland.

Although debt facilities were not due to be renewed until the end of 2013, banks do not hang about if there is a serious danger of a borrower breaching its covenants. New chief executive Mike Clarke, who had already cut the workforce by 600 to reduce costs, spent months persuading the banks to renegotiate the terms of the loan, which was eventually extended to June 2016.

The price was that Premier had to sell off a number of brands, with a share of the cash generated going to the banks, and to concentrate on the eight best sellers. Despite the extension, it was agreed that the debt would be halved in the intervening period.

Premier Foods shares had sunk to just 12p (down from 35p in May 2011) by the time the debt deal was agreed.

## Kitchen sink accounting

You know the expression: everything but the kitchen sink? Struggling companies sometimes throw in the kitchen sink as well, usually when new management is installed to try to rescue an ailing business.

It doesn't mean that the company has branched out into plumbing. What happens is that all the adverse items that can be dredged up are thrown into one set of very poor results in the hope that all the bad news can be got out of the way and things can only get better.

So assets are written down in value to zero, underperforming parts of the group are put up for sale and suddenly have no value, doubtful debts are declared uncollectible, stock is declared unsellable ... anything that can be counted as a loss is thrown in immediately.

This does mean a very poor set of results, probably with a horrendous pre-tax loss, but never mind because it can all be blamed on the old management.

The dividend, if there was one, is also scrapped but that too can be blamed on the outgoing directors.

Next year's results are almost certain to be better, since there are no more nasties to put in. Depreciation will be minimal since as much as possible was thrown into the kitchen sink job last time. If any of those doubtful bills get paid after all, that is a bonus that can be counted into future years' profits.

So even if the second year's results show another loss, as long as it is a smaller loss then the new management can claim that the worst is over (thanks to them, of course).

## Strategic reviews

Companies are particularly keen on strategic reviews. They imply dynamic management seeking to take the business on to greater things and are always announced with a great fanfare.

Investors should not, however, get too carried away. Strategic reviews are popular with new chief executives and may have more to do with the new incumbent's desire to make a mark than to any need for change.

In these cases the review does give the new chief a chance to get to know the business rather than leap prematurely into changing the direction of the company and regretting the haste later.

The review allows fresh ideas to emerge and provides an opportunity for dead wood to be cleared out – just as long as it does not lead to change for the sake of it.

Of rather more concern is when the review indicates that something is seriously wrong with the business, which is why it needs looking at from top to bottom. In the worst case scenario, the review may be needed to avert the impending collapse of the business.

So if you see the announcement that a company has launched a strategic review, read on to find out what it is really all about. As you read, ask yourself why potential improvements to the business have not been spotted sooner.

When the outcome of a strategic review is announced, check that it has real details of proposed action. Be particularly wary of meaningless management speak such as this gem from Lloyds TSB, which headed a fairly meaningless list of must-dos:

---

**OUTCOME OF STRATEGIC REVIEW: KEY HIGHLIGHTS**

"Our aim is to become the best bank for customers. We have around 30 million customers, iconic brands, including Lloyds TSB, Halifax, Bank of Scotland and Scottish Widows, and high-quality, committed people. We will unlock the potential in this franchise over time by creating a simpler, more agile and responsive organisation, and by making substantial investments in better-value products and services for our customers, to deliver strong, stable and sustainable returns for our shareholders."

---

As far as this summary has any meaning, it is simply a list of what we would expect the bank to be doing anyway. To tell us that it aims to be 'the best bank for customers' raises the question of what it has been doing so far.

## Pensions

Much has appeared in the press and on TV on the thorny subject of pensions and the potential black hole that they have created.

Briefly, there are two types of pensions:

1. defined benefits

2. defined contributions

These are described in more detail below.

### 1. Defined benefits

These pension schemes tell employees what benefits they will receive on retirement, typically a percentage of the employee's final salary, and were funded by contributions from employers and employees.

The amount of money that needs to be available is determined by the commitment to pay pensions at a specified level.

It is hard to calculate how much money needs to be in the pot to meet pensions that will be paid many years in the future but while the stock market was booming in the 1980s and 1990s and pension funds were largely invested in shares, nobody much cared. Indeed, companies took pension 'holidays' during which they did not have to contribute to the funds.

After the stock market crash in 2000-3, many pension funds found themselves in deficit and the rules have been tightened to cover the worst case scenario. Companies have not only resumed contributions to these schemes, they have had to throw in extra dollops to fill the hole.

## 2. Defined contributions

In this type of pension the amount of money put into the pot by employer and employee determines the size of the pension at retirement age. This type of fund cannot be in deficit because the size of the pension is determined by the amount of money available, not the other way round as in the defined benefits scheme.

Naturally companies have been busy scrapping their defined benefits schemes and substituting defined contributions schemes. In some cases existing employees are allowed to keep their perks and the new scheme applies only to new employees; in other cases even existing employees have been forced to switch.

### Why a pension deficit matters

These pension deficits are important to you as an investor for two main reasons. Where companies are saddled with a bill for filling up the hole, they will suffer from correspondingly reduced profits for several years until the hole is filled.

Companies do publish valuations of their pension fund assets and liabilities as calculated by specialists (known as actuaries) so you can see the size of any deficit. They will also report in their results how much extra they are putting in and how many years they expect to take to fill the hole.

---

## Case study: BT

The telecoms provider was saddled with Britain's largest private sector pension plan, a plan that at one stage had a black hole of £9 billion that plagued BT for years. It was so serious that BT actually went to court in 2010 to secure a ruling that in the last resort the government, which had once owned BT before it was privatised, was responsible for the deficit.

The final salary scheme was closed to new members in 2001 but that still left about 350,000 employees and former employees entitled to a pension based on their final salary.

BT did set about reducing the deficit, agreeing with the pension fund trustees that it would pay £525 million a year into the scheme. It could afford to do so because it had surplus cash generated by the business.

At the end of 2011, BT had £1.5 billion in cash and investments generating minimal returns and was expected to generate another £2.4 billion cash in the year to the end of March. From this cash BT decided to pay £2 billion into the pension fund immediately to minimise the shadow hanging over it. At that stage the deficit was down to just over £4 billion.

This cash could have been handed to shareholders in the form of dividends or share buybacks so the pension drain was a serious handicap from the investor's point of view.

---

## Pensions and bids

The pension deficit can also be of crucial importance when a company attracts interest from a potential bidder. The trustees of the pension fund have a duty to ensure that anyone buying the company has also got the finances to make up any pension fund deficit.

This can be particularly important if the bid approach has come from a venture capital consortium because these are almost invariably loaded up with debt to pay for the proposed acquisition.

Pension fund trustees can in effect have the power to block takeovers as they carry out their duties to protect pension fund members.

---

### Case study: British Airways

Issues over a pension deficit cropped up not just once but twice as obstacles to the UK flag carrier as it sought to expand as a word leader.

First, BA set up a merger with Spanish airline Iberia. One stumbling block was BA's £3.7 billion pension fund deficit. Even after the merger was agreed, Iberia retained the right to walk away unless the pension deficit was addressed. The issue was resolved to the satisfaction of the pension fund trustees by BA agreeing to top up the fund to the tune of £330 million a year for 16 years.

Soon after the merger, the newly formed International Airlines Group (IAG) took a fancy to buying BMI, a British carrier that was owned by German airline Lufthansa. BMI was loss making and IAG wanted it only for the landing slots at Heathrow. The big question as far as the trustees were concerned was who would take responsibility for BMI's £180 million pension fund deficit.

---

## Time will tell

This pensions issue will gradually go away over time. The switch to defined contribution schemes will eliminate the danger of black holes in the future as the problem is effectively passed from the company to its employees, who simply get smaller pensions.

In addition, the extra contributions from the companies into existing defined benefit schemes, plus the rising values of investments, should eventually eliminate or at least alleviate the deficits.

# SECTION D
Investing

# Chapter 14
## Starting Out

### First – study yourself

It can be a daunting prospect to invest in the stock market for the first time so it is very important to do your homework. Start by studying yourself.

Only you know what you can afford to invest, what risks you want to take or can afford to take, whether you want to invest for the short or long term and whether you want a steady stream of income to live on or to store up wealth for the future.

Before you invest, sit down with pen and paper and note your income and all your outgoings, including food, clothing, entertainment and holidays as well as any mortgage payments, utility bills and any monthly instalments on furniture or electrical appliances.

You should consider owning your own home if you are renting. Like shares, property values can fall but they also rise over the long term and you have to live somewhere.

Most families these days own a car. If you do, you should allocate some cash towards the next one.

Indeed, you may feel more comfortable with some of your cash invested in liquid assets, that is money you can get hold of in an emergency at little or no notice such as savings in a building society account.

Shares are liquid in that they can be sold quickly in the stock market but there is always the danger that you find yourself having to sell just when the market is depressed. Keeping a pot of cash earning some interest but readily available gives you the leeway to hang on to shares that you believe will gain value and can then be sold at a higher price.

If you decide, despite reading this book, that you need the help of a financial adviser you must lay your soul bare. The adviser needs to know all your financial circumstances and your investment aims in order to give you the advice that suits you.

In the following chapters we will look at different investment strategies but first there are some general points worth noting.

## Keep yourself informed

You don't have to sit at your computer screen watching share price movements all day. Leave that for the day traders, the people who make a living by buying in the morning and selling a few hours later.

You should, however, keep abreast of what is going on. Information is freely available in newspapers, specialist magazines and financial websites so there is no excuse for burying your head in the sand.

We noted in the section on companies that they are required to issue at least two announcements each year: the interim results and the full year results. These are usually accompanied by an indication of how trading is going.

In addition, companies now issue quarterly trading statements to fill in the gaps between the half yearly results so you are less likely to find that disaster has struck out of the blue.

In 2007, as part of the drive to ensure that companies keep shareholders fully informed, the European Union issued the Transparency Directive, so named because it is supposed to enable you to see right through the company.

UK companies with a full listing must now issue a trading update, called an interim management statement, after the first and third quarters of their financial years to supplement information issued alongside the half year and final results.

This ruling does not apply to companies with a quotation on AIM.

## Factors that affect share prices

Share prices are on the move throughout the trading day. Those of the largest companies such as BP and Vodafone will change moment by moment as buying and selling ebbs and flows; those of the tiniest companies may move only sporadically and may go for several days without a change.

The main impetus for share price change is supply and demand. When buyers pile in, shares inevitably go up; a flood of sellers is bound to depress the market.

However, buying and selling pressure is the symptom rather than the cause. We need to look at why it is sometimes predominantly buyers and sometimes sellers who are out in force. We should note that on some days practically the whole market moves in one direction while at other times it is just particular sectors and sometimes just individual shares selectively.

Even when the market as a whole is moving in one direction, perhaps over a prolonged period, some shares will buck the trend. During the three year bear market in 2000-2003, when Footsie shares on average lost more than half their value, oil explorer Soco and financial broker ICAP both saw their shares increase by more than 400%.

### Market movements

#### Reasons why the market as a whole moves

1. There is new UK economic news such as inflation figures.

2. Markets around the world are moving in a particular way and London joins the trend. Shares here are particularly influenced by

large movements on the New York Stock Exchange as the US is the world's largest economy.

3. The market has moved strongly in one particular direction and investors take profits or look for bargains.

4. The world economy takes a turn for the better or worse.

### Reasons why a sector moves

1. There is news specific to that sector, for instance a rise in oil prices will hit the shares of transport companies faced with higher fuel bills.

2. Sales of goods and services in one sector are affected by changes in consumer behaviour, such as the switch from high street shopping to buying on the internet.

3. Companies in a particular sector are expected to be involved in takeover activity.

### Reasons why shares in a particular company move

1. Sales and profits are better or worse than expected.

2. The company announces that it expects to beat or fall short of analysts' expectations.

3. A rival company is winning its business or is struggling to keep its own share of the market.

4. Rumours about the company circulate, particularly if the talk is of a takeover.

5. A takeover or an approach that could lead to a bid is announced.

6. There are changes to senior management.

7. Directors buy or sell shares in the company.

8. The board changes its strategy, perhaps deciding to seek new markets, expand overseas or sell loss making operations.

These are all logical reasons for share price movements, but it is also true that the stock market can, in the short term, be an irrational place and rises and falls sometimes seem to defy logic. Such movements are prompted by market *sentiment,* the general feeling in the market.

Shares may start to rise and punters leap onto the bandwagon for fear of missing an opportunity, only to fall off painfully when the bandwagon comes to an abrupt halt. Then shares may fall back sharply in what is known as a correction.

## Interest rates

### Why and how interest rates move

Interest rates used to be set by the Chancellor of the Exchequer and changes tended to come out of the blue. But one of the first things that Gordon Brown did when he moved into No. 11 Downing Street was to put the Bank of England in charge of interest rates.

The Bank has a Monetary Policy Committee (MPC) of nine men and women comprising the Governor of the Bank of England, the Deputy Governor, other senior Bank of England staff and outsiders appointed by the Chancellor. Its task is to keep inflation within prescribed limits, currently between 1% and 3% as measured by the Consumer Price Index.

Interest rates run in cycles, rising and falling over a period of months or years. Mercifully for investors the Bank tries to warn us of impending changes in interest rates and to give some idea of where we are in the cycle so there is no reason to get caught out.

The MPC meets early in each month and members vote on whether to raise rates, keep them as they are or reduce them. The majority vote prevails and if necessary the Governor has a casting vote. The decision is announced at noon on a Thursday.

Changes are normally a quarter point in either direction, although individual members have occasionally voted for half point changes and sometimes larger movements do happen. Minutes of the meeting, including voting figures, are issued later in the month. The Bank also issues a quarterly report so there are plenty of clues as to how the wind is blowing.

In broad terms, interest rates are likely to be raised when inflation rises above the 2% midpoint in the target range. Higher interest rates make debt more expensive, demand for goods is curtailed and consumers start to get twitchy. It becomes more attractive to save than to spend.

Interest rates are likely to be lowered when inflation falls below the 2% midpoint. Lower interest rates make debt less expensive so consumers are more inclined to go out and spend. Saving becomes less attractive.

These general rules were cast aside when stimulating an economic recovery after the credit crunch took precedence over controlling inflation but they still apply in principle.

### The effect of interest rates on share prices

Share prices are affected by changes in interest rates:

- rising interest rates are bad news and send share prices lower;
- falling interest rates are good news and send share prices higher.

Several reasons why higher interest rates are bad for shares are:

- If demand for goods and services falls (as consumers have less cash to spend), then companies will make reduced profits.
- The pound becomes more attractive for foreign investors to hold, so sterling rises on the foreign exchange market and British goods become more expensive abroad, so exports are affected.
- Companies that export from the UK or have operations abroad find that their profits are reduced when foreign currency is converted into more expensive pounds.

- Investors find it is more attractive to invest in bonds or even keep their cash on deposit because they are now being paid a higher rate of interest.

- Investors who take the risk of borrowing money to buy shares find it more expensive to do so.

- Preference shares fall in value because the fixed rate of interest becomes less attractive.

Rising interest rates are referred to as a tightening of monetary policy.

When inflation falls the Bank of England can relax or ease monetary policy by cutting interest rates. Now the factors we considered when discussing rising interest rates work in reverse. Consumers spend more and save less, which is generally good for the profits of UK companies. Bonds become less attractive, while borrowing money to buy shares offers a better hope of producing a decent profit.

Thus falling interest rates tend to push share prices higher.

## Facing reality

We should not panic if shares in a company fall just after we have invested in it. We should reconsider whether the reasons for our purchase still hold. If we are still confident of the investment case, the lower share price actually makes the case stronger because the shares are now more of a bargain.

However, the hardest thing for any investor to do is put hand on heart and admit: 'I got it wrong'. Even hardened professionals cling to shares as the price falls relentlessly in the vain belief that their precious investment must eventually prove justified.

None of us get it right all the time and sometimes you will have to bite the bullet and sell at a loss.

Some investors set a stop loss. They fix a price at 10% or 20% below the price at which they buy a particular share and resolve to sell if the share falls to that level. In that way any losses are limited.

There is no magic level at which you should set your stop loss. Set it too high and you will sell out before you have given the shares a real chance to perform. Set it too low and you risk a heavier fall if you really have picked a loser. You need to decide what your attitude will be before you invest.

# Chapter 15
## Stockbrokers

You will need a stockbroker who is a member of the London Stock Exchange to carry out the transaction for you when you buy or sell shares. A broker is a go-between, in this case between you and the stock market.

Some large banks offer a dealing service to their customers so you can ask the bank where you have your current or savings account what facilities, if any, are available. The advantage is that you probably wander into your local branch from time to time to draw out cash or pay bills so you are likely to feel comfortable making an enquiry there.

You can buy with cash directly out of your account so there is no need to set up a new one.

The big drawback is that you may have to deal at best price, that is instruct the bank to buy or sell at whatever price it can get rather than have the flexibility to stipulate the price at which you are willing to deal.

The alternative, which need not be daunting, is to set up an account with a stockbroker. There is no shortage of them and wherever you live you should be able to find one in a town or city near your home, although in these days of mass communications this is not necessary.

Many people, though, do prefer to deal with an office that they can visit and meet a staff member to get a feel for the place and discuss their requirements. That way they will be a face, not just a name.

The London Stock Exchange website (**www.londonstockexchange.com**) has a full list of approved stockbrokers. Look at the bottom of the home page for the column headed 'Tools and services' and select 'Locate a Broker'. This takes you to the website page:

**www.londonstockexchange.com/exchange/prices-and-markets/stocks/tools-and-services/find-a-broker-search.html**

You can call up a list of brokers providing the type of service you want.

Or you can approach the Association of Private Client Investment Managers and Stockbrokers, an organisation that represents the overwhelming majority of brokers and investment advisers in Britain.

The APCIMS website (**www.apcims.co.uk**) not only has a list of stockbrokers but a search facility so you can narrow the list down to brokers in your area, those willing to handle your size of investment and the types of services you want.

The relevant web page is:

**www.apcims.co.uk/about-apcims/apcims-members**

You will be looking for a stockbroker who is happy to handle small clients, so don't start looking for the biggest names in the business. They probably won't want your account unless you are particularly wealthy.

If you are happy using the internet, there are online brokers. They tend to be geared to small accounts and they tend to be cheap.

Best of all is to find a friend or acquaintance who already has a stockbroker. If they are happy with the service they are getting, word of mouth counts for as much in this sphere as it does in finding a handyman or an electrician.

Decide how much you want to invest, either a lump sum or a regular investment, and tell the broker at the outset so you are quite sure they handle your size of account.

Some, but not all, brokers offer services such as self-invested pension plans (Sipps) and individual savings accounts (ISAs).

Now you must decide what kind of service you require.

## Execution only

You take all the decisions. You decide what shares you want to buy or sell and your broker will quote the current price so you can decide whether to go ahead or not. When you buy shares you need to decide how much to invest in each company and calculate how many shares you will get for that amount of money.

If you are confident after reading this book, this is the service for you. You put in your order and the stockbroker buys or sells according to your instructions.

## Advisory services

You still make your own decisions and the stockbroker will buy and sell only on your say-so but this time the stockbroker provides expert advice and guidance. Naturally you have to pay extra for the advice.

You should receive research notes produced by the brokers' analysts and advice tailored to your specific needs.

Charges vary from broker to broker so you will have to shop around. Given the vast number of stocks on the London Stock Exchange, you cannot expect your broker to cover every single one. Some brokers specialise in covering larger or smaller companies, others look at a fixed range of specific sectors. Always ask before you commit yourself.

## Discretionary management

You hand over your cash and the stockbroker takes the decisions for you. The broker has the authority to make investment decisions without your prior approval.

You will need to make it clear what your investment objectives are, for example whether you want income or capital gains and whether you want to play as safe as possible or how much risk you are willing to take.

## Direct Market Access

This is a new and growing service that lets investors execute trades directly with other market participants on the LSE's trading services. Direct market access is more widespread in the US. Generally, it is more useful to short-term traders than investors. It is therefore probably best for new investors to trade through traditional methods first.

## Confidentiality

Whichever service you decide to take, your stockbroker is under an obligation to keep your financial affairs confidential. This does mean that you can make a full and frank disclosure of your financial position without fear it will fall into the hands of the tabloid newspapers.

If you want advice from your stockbroker you must be completely open, otherwise the advice cannot be tailored to your requirements.

## Costs

### Commissions

The days of fixed commissions set by the London Stock Exchange have long since gone and brokers are free to set their own charges. Inevitably they will be restricted by the knowledge that rival brokers will undercut them if they charge too much.

The price of the service you select will vary from broker to broker, perhaps enormously.

Execution only is the cheapest, as you are doing all the real work. You will be charged so much per trade, either a fixed amount or a percentage of the value of the transaction. Expect to find that there is a minimum charge.

It can cost as little as £5 per trade and you might even get a special offer as a new customer.

Advisory services may levy a charge per trade, an annual fee or a mixture of both. Check how many analysts' notes you are entitled to per year.

For a discretionary service you will usually pay an annual fee, probably larger than for the advisory service as the broker is doing all the work. There could also be a charge per transaction so do give your broker clear instructions to avoid churn, making more buys and sells than necessary.

Your broker should not churn your account but if you feel that the number of deals being made are excessive, find another broker. The broker has discretion but not total control. You can stipulate, for example, that shares in a particular company must not be sold or that you do not want investments in companies you regard as unethical.

The broker should be prepared to set out the fees clearly and it is imperative that you ask what you are going to be charged. The money comes out of your investment pot.

### Stamp duty

With all trades you will, unfortunately, have to pay stamp duty of 0.5% of the value of the transaction on all share purchases, though not on sales. Campaigns over many years to get this imposition removed have fallen on deaf ears. No wonder. The Chancellor of the Exchequer raises £3bn a year from stamp duty on share purchases.

You do not pay stamp duty on purchases of shares quoted on overseas exchanges. So although your broker will probably charge extra for dealing on an overseas exchange you will recoup the difference by avoiding stamp duty.

## Cold callers – a warning

You should deal only with reputable stockbrokers registered with the Financial Services Authority. In particular, you should be extremely suspicious of cold callers, the complete strangers who ring you on the telephone out of the blue.

The FSA has on its website (**www.fsa.gov.uk**) a list of known operators that are not kosher but the list is far from exhaustive. It cannot be, as dubious operations and outright crooks simply change their names once they are rumbled.

Although many pretend to be British operations with UK addresses, they are more likely to be working from Amsterdam or Barcelona and you will have no legal protection and no hope of compensation if you are fleeced. That UK address is probably a mailing address, not a real office.

Nor should you assume that a country such as Switzerland, with its reputation of strict financial rules, will look after your interests in preference to those of a Swiss national if push comes to shove.

The myriad ploys designed to part the gullible from their money are sufficiently numerous and fascinating to fill a book on their own but the general principle is that you are lumbered with an 'investment' that is unsellable, in sharp contrast to the London Stock Exchange which is all about creating a market for the mutual benefit of buyers and sellers alike.

A particular ploy is to offer shares in a company that is unquoted but which is supposedly coming to market soon. You are assured that the shares will soar when they are floated. It's all promises, most of them meaningless.

Ask yourself this: If something is too good to be true, why would you believe it?

# Chapter 16
## Fundamental Data

There are three ways of deciding which shares to invest in:

1. fundamental data

2. charting

3. gut feeling

The best policy may be to take a combination of the three and the more you invest the better your judgement will become. Fundamentals are based on hard facts about the company; charting follows movements in the company's share price; gut feeling is something that cannot be easily defined or taught.

If you get a feeling that a company is heading for trouble or is about to turn the corner, and you find that nine times out of ten you are right, by all means follow your heart. Otherwise it is probably best to stick with what is more tangible.

Fundamentals are the figures that the company puts out in its profit and loss account and in its balance sheet plus the calculations that you can make with those figures.

Through the fundamentals you can work out whether shares look good value.

## Historic and prospective data

Figures published by the company cover periods of time that have elapsed. Their main advantage is that they are real figures. They tell you what really happened but they are historic. They do not in themselves tell you what will happen over the coming months.

Analysts employed by stockbrokers make forecasts covering up to 24 months ahead. These forecasts are referred to as prospective or forward. They have the big advantage of telling you what is likely to happen to revenue and profits so you can assess how share prices will be affected in the future. However, they are only forecasts, not actual figures, and they can be wrong.

Larger companies are researched by several analysts and it is possible to get a consensus or average view of expectations. Smaller companies may be researched by only one or two analysts, or there may be no forecasts at all.

On balance it is better to rely on prospective data because you are buying shares for future, not past, earnings but there is no reason why you should not consider past and forecast earnings when making investments.

# Ratios

There are two particularly important pieces of fundamental data that you should consider when deciding to buy a company's shares: dividend yield and the price/earnings ratio.

## Dividend yield

The yield is particularly important if you are looking for steady income from your shares.

Do not assume that large dividends in terms of pence per share are necessarily more attractive. If the shares are more expensive then you need a bigger dividend to make the investment worthwhile.

Let us suppose that the shares in company A cost you 100p and the company pays a dividend of 4p. For every £100 you put in, you get 100 shares and the dividend you receive will amount to £4. The yield is 4%, that is £4 on every £100 invested.

Shares in company B cost 200p each and the dividend is 5p. Although the dividend is 1p higher than at company A, the yield is only 2.5%.

For every £100 you invest, you get only 50 shares so you receive only £2.50 in dividends. The yield is therefore 2.5%, or £2.50 for every £100 invested.

You can calculate the yield on any share quite simply by dividing the dividend by the price of the shares. Remember that both figures must be in pence (or, if appropriate, in euros or US dollars) so you are dividing like with like.

You can use the historic figure to get the historic yield or analysts' forecasts to calculate the prospective yield.

The following table gives examples of companies and their historic and forecast dividend yields in March 2012.

Table 17: sample historic and forecast dividend yields

| Company | Share price | Dividend | Yield | Forecast dividend | Prospective yield |
|---------|-------------|----------|-------|-------------------|-------------------|
| United Utilities | 618p | 30p | 4.9% | 32p | 5.2% |
| Rentokil | 84.5p | 1.33p | 1.6% | 2.08p | 2.5% |
| Ladbroke | 156p | 7.8p | 5.0% | 8.03p | 5.1% |
| Tesco | 331.5p | 14.46p | 4.4% | 15.0p | 4.5% |
| Capita | 736.5p | 21.4p | 2.95% | 23.42p | 3.2% |

Sources: London Stock Exchange, Morningstar

We can see that although all five companies are expected to increase their dividend the effect on the yield varies. Only a modest improvement in yield is forecast for Ladbroke and Tesco; Capita and United Utilities are seen as making a noticeable step up; while Rentokil with the smallest yield is set to show the biggest improvement.

The higher the yield, the greater your income for every pound invested. You may wonder why some companies have much higher or lower yields or dividends than average.

Companies look cheap when there are doubts about how well they will fare in the future while others look expensive because the market sees them as good investments that are highly likely to grow in value.

If there are reasonable hopes that the dividend will continue to rise for the foreseeable future, then investors may be happy with a low but solid yield. Where there are serious doubts about a company's profits and the possibility arises that the dividend will have to be cut in future, then investors will want a higher yield in the meantime to compensate for the extra risk.

Remember, the stock market is about risks and rewards. The greater the risk, the greater the reward you are entitled to expect if it all comes right in the end.

## Price/earnings ratio

The second vital figure, particularly relevant to those looking for capital gains rather than income, is the price/earnings ratio, often referred to as the rating because it indicates whether the shares look cheap or expensive.

This ratio (usually abbreviated to PER or just PE) is calculated by dividing the price of the shares by the earnings per share after tax.

As with yield, you must divide pence by pence or euros by euros. But unlike the yield, where you get a better return from a higher figure, the price-earnings ratio identifies cheap shares as the ones with a lower figure. The lower the PE, the cheaper the share.

Also, as with the yield, a historic PER can be calculated from historic earnings per share, while a forecast PER can be calculated from forecast earnings per share.

The following table gives the same companies we used to illustrate yield to provide examples of historic and forecast PERs, again in March 2012.

Table 18: sample historic and forecast PERs

| Company | Share price | Earnings | PER | Projected earnings | Projected PER |
|---|---|---|---|---|---|
| United Utilities | 618p | 35.10p | 17.6 | 35.15p | 17.6 |
| Rentokil | 84.5p | 7.48p | 11.3 | 8.36p | 10.1 |
| Ladbroke | 156p | 15.00p | 10.4 | 16.19p | 9.6 |
| Tesco | 331.5p | 35.90p | 9.2 | 34.38p | 9.6 |
| Capita | 736.5p | 48.49p | 15.2 | 52.42p | 14.0 |

Sources: London Stock Exchange, Morningstar

We can see that at the point when we took our figures Rentokil, Ladbroke and Capita were expected to improve earnings and therefore the prospective PER was lower than the historic figure; United Utilities was set to remain on a comparatively high rating; and Tesco was in danger of suffering a fall in earnings, and therefore a rise in its PER.

Generally, companies growing quickly tend to have high PE ratios, while slow growth companies have low ratings. Certain industries (e.g. technology related) tend to be regarded as high growth and therefore attract high ratings; whereas other industries (e.g. utilities) are traditionally viewed as low growth and have low ratings. Companies in the same industry tend to have similar ratings. However, anomalies do occur and, as with the yield, a company's rating may look cheap for good reason. A lowly rating can indicate concern over the company's prospects, while a high rating reflects confidence.

# Chapter 17
## Charting

Chartists believe that shares gain a momentum that may or may not be justified by fundamental data.

We can see when a company is theoretically under or overvalued. The stock market can be particularly efficient at ironing out these kinks, so in theory a share price should not get far out of line before the laws of supply and demand pull it back into place.

However, the stock market can be an irrational place, running at least in part on what is referred to as sentiment, the overall feeling of investors towards particular shares or the market place in general.

If shares start to move in a particular direction, investors jump on the bandwagon, sometimes in simple fear of missing out. The stampede can turn into a panic.

Chartists look for trends in the share price chart. They are right to say that once a share starts to move in a particular direction the trend often continues for much longer than investors expect. Private investors are particularly fond of grabbing profits too soon, selling out long before the share price rise is over, yet they cling to falling shares rather than admit they made a bad choice.

Charting is a highly specialised art and this book will deal only with the basics. Charting does not supply sure-fire tips for success, otherwise everyone would be doing it. Critics would say that, as with any other method of stock picking, the only certainty is that it tells you after the event what you should have done last week or last month.

The mantras of charting are that you go with the flow and the trend is your friend. As a general principle, chartists are willing to miss out on the early opportunities for buying on the cheap. They do not try to catch falling shares as they hit the bottom or to set the momentum going. They jump on the bandwagon once it is moving and enjoy the ride, hoping to get off just before it all comes to an end.

They look for those occasions when a share chart starts to draw a pretty picture and we will cover some of the key indications. Note that the principles of charting apply not just to individual shares. We can apply them to market sectors or to the whole market. So we could, for example, study trends for banks or house builders and we could look at the FTSE 100 or the AIM UK 50.

We can discuss here only the basic concept of charting. It is possible to write a whole book on the subject, or even on just one aspect of charting. People have done so.

## Floors and ceilings

Chartists look for support points, a level in a particular share price where investors have in the past been tempted to buy, sending the shares higher. This is also known as a floor.

They are also wary of resistance levels or ceilings, points in the chart where shareholders have previously decided to take profits because they believed that the shares would not go any higher.

Note that, with all lines that chartists draw, it is rare for the share price to consistently touch a trend line exactly, which is why chartists usually want to see a line broken decisively before they are satisfied that a new phase has begun.

Chart 7: Legal & General, examples of support and resistance levels

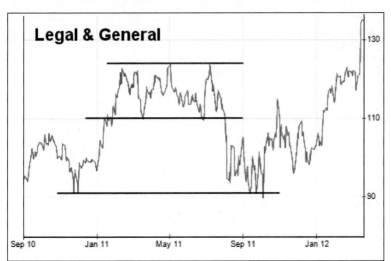

Having broken upwards, Legal & General shares peaked at just above 120p, and four attempts to break up to 125p failed as selling resistance kicked in each time. On the way up, 110p had briefly provided a ceiling. As so often happens, when this ceiling was broken quickly and decisively it became a new floor, with buyers coming out in support on two occasions when the shares fell back.

In time this floor gave way, and the shares promptly retreated to find support at around 93p, which had been the support level before the upward break.

## Rangebound

An extension of the concept of support and resistance levels is that sometimes share prices move sideways, bouncing up and down between two levels. When this happens chartists are looking to see which way the shares break out, upwards or downwards, so that a new trend is established.

Chart 8: Persimmon

**Persimmon**

House builders saw their shares fall heavily in 2008 and early 2009 as the credit crunch bit and mortgages became extremely hard to obtain. First time buyers were virtually squeezed out of the market. However, by the middle of 2009 the fall had run its course and house builders' shares generally went nowhere for the best part of three years.

Persimmon was typical of the pattern, finding support each time the shares edged below 350p and running into profit taking just above 500p. The decisive break came on the upside and once the ceiling was broken the shares surged to 700p.

## Narrowing triangles

A variation on shares moving within set ceilings and floors is where the range grows ever narrower. Again, chartists will be looking to see in which direction the shares break out, only this time we can see when crunch time is looming.

Chart 9: Highland Gold

We can see that the peaks are getting gradually lower while the troughs are rising sharply. At some point in February 2012 the two lines were set to meet and something had to give. In this instance it was the support level that was broken and the shares fell back heavily in the following weeks.

## Peaks and troughs

Shares do not run in straight lines up or down. Even on a good bull run there will be occasional small falls among the rises as some investors decide to take profits. Similarly, falling shares will perk up from time to time, as buyers provide support, before resuming their bear trend.

We can, however, gain clues from looking at whether each peak is lower or higher than the previous one or whether each trough is lower or higher than before. For as long as such a pattern holds we would expect the established trend to continue.

Chart 10: share price of Admiral

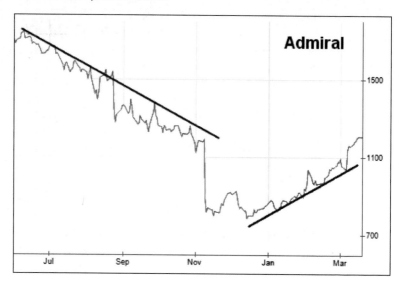

We can see that throughout the summer and into the autumn of 2011, insurance group Admiral was on a declining trend with peaks and troughs forming at an ever lower level. Two peaks did emerge above the trend line in August, though only marginally so, and the next peak in September fell short of the line but the general trend was maintained until Admiral shares fell over the edge of a cliff in November.

In December, however, a new trend emerged. Now the shares set off on an upward trend, with each peak and trough higher than the previous ones. The chart tells us that the shares had turned the corner and a new phase was intact.

When you see such a chart, draw a straight line joining as far as possible all the peaks and all the troughs. If each peak is higher than the previous peak, and if each trough is higher than the previous one, then the bull phase is still intact.

In the case of a rising share price, the troughs are more important than the peaks. The troughs mark the point at which buyers again outnumbered the sellers who were getting out, the point at which the shares found support. As long as the shares stay above the rising support line, they are still in a bull phase. When the share price drops below the line, it can be a signal to get out.

When shares are falling, with each peak below the previous peak and each trough below the previous trough, the shares are in a bear phase. This time the peaks are more important. They represent the falling level at which buyers lose enthusiasm and the sellers take over again.

If the shares rise above the line connecting the peaks, it is a signal that the bear phase could be over and it could be time to buy.

Note the words can and could. There is no guarantee that the trend is broken, just a strong indication. Share charts do not move in regular patterns so those straight lines cannot exactly touch every peak and trough spot on.

# Chapter 18
## Tips

## Stockbroker analysts

Several stockbrokers employ analysts who pronounce on the merits or otherwise of companies with stock market quotations.

These analysts are required to pass examinations in order to register with the Financial Services Authority before they are allowed to make recommendations. The stockbrokers they work for will also be registered with the FSA and are required to ensure compliance with strict rules, particularly in terms of avoiding a conflict of interest.

Each analyst will cover a specific sector to build up expertise and each broker will cover a limited range of companies or sectors, or may specialise in covering just larger or only smaller companies. With nearly 2,000 companies quoted on the London Stock Exchange, including AIM companies, it would need quite an army to research and report on the lot.

Analysts do have access to directors of companies that they cover, especially when results are announced. Companies may hold analysts' briefings to answer questions arising from results or trading statements. They may take them on site visits; say to a manufacturing facility or a retail outlet.

However, companies are not allowed to pass sensitive information to analysts in private. Anything that might affect the share price must be put into the public domain.

Apart from their specialised knowledge and expertise in reading company accounts and balance sheets, analysts have more time than most private investors to study all the details and to offer a considered assessment. It is, after all, their job. They are, though, human and like all experts they can get it wrong.

Analysts draw up reports on the companies they cover, assess strengths and weaknesses and make forecasts of turnover and profits for the current financial year and the next one.

They will make recommendations on whether investors should buy or sell the shares. These reports are sent privately to the stockbroker's clients who have paid for the service. It is only fair that those who have paid up get first go at the assessment but a summary of the week's recommendations appears in various weekend newspapers as well as the *Investors Chronicle* and *Shares* magazine.

## Interpretation of analysts' recommendations

The recommendations can be confusing because the terminology varies between brokers but generally they work on a scale from one to five, ranging from a confident buy recommendation, a less enthusiastic but still positive stance, a neutral position, a fairly negative position and a clear sell recommendation.

For clarity the table below sets out most of the different expressions used.

Table 19: terminology of analysts' recommendations

| Hot | Lukewarm | Tepid | Chilly | Freezing |
|---|---|---|---|---|
| Strong buy | Buy | Hold | Sell | Strong sell |
| Buy | Add | Hold | Reduce | Sell |
| Buy | Overweight | Neutral | Underweight | Sell |
| Strong buy | Weak buy | Neutral | Weak sell | Strong sell |
| Buy | Outperform | Market performer | Underperform | Sell |

You may wonder how it is possible to have different grades of buy or sell recommendations. Surely a buy is a buy and a sell is a sell?

Also confusing is that some analysts use 'buy' at the top end of the scale while others do not, and likewise they may or may not put 'sell' at the bottom of the scale. The lines can get a little blurred.

You would be quite right to raise such objections. Analysts, like the rest of us, can be mealy mouthed and hedge their bets. All you can assume is that analysts making a half hearted buy or sell recommendation feel less sure they are right than if they went the whole hog.

The implication with a weak buy is that you should buy some shares but not too many. With a weak sell you could sell some but not all of your holdings. This intention is more clear when add and reduce are used.

The terms overweight and underweight cause confusion. The analyst is suggesting that you should hold more or fewer shares in a particular company than you normally would. For example, if you tend to invest £2,000 in each company in your portfolio, overweight would imply buying say £2,500 worth while underweight would steer you to risking only £1,500.

Outperform, market performer and underperform are a bit of a cop-out. Instead of recommending whether you should buy or sell the shares, the analyst is assessing how they will fare in comparison with the rest of the stock market.

Supposing the market is steady, with little movement on the FTSE 100 or other indices. Then 'outperform' stocks will rise and 'underperform' stocks will fall if the analyst is right.

But if the stock market rises then even the 'underperform' stocks are likely to rise: they will just rise less than the rest of the market. In these circumstances an analyst can claim to have been right if an 'underperform' stock shows a modest rise.

Similarly if the stock market tumbles then even an outperforming stock can fall back.

As a general rule, treat 'outperform' as a buy indication and 'underperform' as a sell rating but view them with more caution than an outright recommendation.

Analysts may also advise investors to avoid a particular stock. Well, that at least is perfectly clear: don't buy the shares and if you already hold them sell them pronto. This is the strongest 'sell' recommendation of all, implying that you should not touch the shares with a bargepole.

Another recommendation occasionally seen is take profits, which is similar to 'sell' but with a subtle difference. A 'sell' recommendation implies that the company is doing badly; 'take profits' means that the shares have had a good run. The company is probably still in good shape; it is just that the shares have run up a little too quickly and might fall back to a more realistic level.

Finally, we occasionally see shares labelled as fair value or up with events. This is an alternative version of 'hold' or neutral' and indicates that the market has got this one about right. In the view of the analysts there are no compelling reasons to buy or sell these shares.

## Can analysts be trusted?

So, analysts are experts but can we trust them? After all, the stockbrokers they work for are touting for trade among the companies they write about. Surely they are under pressure to be nice, especially to companies that are employing their colleagues as advisers.

There has been heavy criticism in the past over the role of analysts. Stockbrokers were supposed to operate what were called Chinese Walls between different parts of their business, with analysts blissfully unaware which companies their colleagues were advising or buying shares in.

Imaginary walls as thick as the Great Wall of China would not prevent information seeping through. This notion was as ludicrous as the Great Wall of China itself and proved just as useless, though both were erected at great expense.

Over the years the situation has improved. Analysts do declare prominently on their research notes when they work for the house stockbroker, that is the broker retained to act for the company. Some brokers will issue research on companies where they are house broker but avoid making recommendations.

You should certainly err on the side of scepticism when reading research. In the case of house brokers you should consider whether recommendations ought to be downgraded one or two levels, assuming that 'buy' should really read 'hold' and 'hold' should read 'sell'. I cannot remember ever seeing a sell recommendation from a house broker.

Analysts at different stockbrokers can and do take different views of the same company. No-one, not even the experts, gets it right all the time. Usually it is a difference between 'buy' from one analyst and 'hold' from another or between 'hold' and 'sell' but occasionally one analyst sees the stock as a buy and another advises selling.

You may have noticed these occasional discrepancies in one of the Saturday or Sunday newspapers that summarise brokers' tips.

You must, as always, use your own judgement. Try to assess whose arguments seem more convincing. Keep a note of these clashes and check later how the shares of the company in question fared. You may get a feel for which stockbroker tends to get it right more often.

Analysts tend to make far more buy recommendations than sell, as the former tends to generate more orders. Also they don't win business from a company by telling investors to sell its shares!

## Newspapers and magazines

The financial pages of the newspapers are excellent ways to keep in touch with events on the stock market and the economy in general. You probably buy a newspaper anyway so the City pages come free.

Do try taking different papers, both on weekdays and on Sunday, to get a feel for which provides the level of City coverage that suits you.

Not all provide share tips. Among the dailies, Tempus in *The Times*, Questor in *The Daily Telegraph* and The Investment Column in *The Independent* offer share tips. For the Sundays, Midas in the Mail on Sunday and Share Tips in *The Sunday Telegraph* tip individual shares. *The Sunday Times* has allowed one or two tips to creep into its Business section but it remains wary of making outright recommendations.

There are two weekly magazines with tips columns: the *Investors Chronicle*, published on Fridays, offers Mr Bearbull, while *Shares* magazine comes out on Thursdays and carries Plays of the Week. Both these magazines may carry tips in other sections.

The two magazines and some weekend newspapers also carry summaries of tips from stockbrokers.

Unlike analysts, financial journalists are unlikely to have passed any examination for registration with the Financial Services Authority, nor will the newspapers they write for be supervised by the FSA.

The Financial Services Act 1996 specifically absolved newspapers from the regulatory regime unless they were tip sheets – that is, they specifically existed to tip shares. We have seen since then the gradual disappearance or scaling back of share tipping from some publications to avoid attracting the attentions of the FSA.

Newspapers therefore do not have to comply with stricter rules on matters such as avoiding a conflict of interest; any rules that are followed are voluntary ones set by the newspaper. This is unlikely to go beyond expecting any journalist writing on a company to declare to the City Editor any shareholding he or she has in that company.

Nonetheless, tip columns are edited by, and largely written by, financial journalists specialising in this field. I have written for three of the publications listed above and can vouch for the general integrity of their tips columns (though I will leave the readers to decide on their general success).

As with the analysts working for stockbrokers, you can find conflicting advice in newspaper tips columns. Once again, investors must use their own judgement to decide which arguments seem more convincing and which tipsters tend to get it right most of the time. Newspaper tipsters mercifully tend to be clearer and simpler in their categories of advice. You will mainly find 'buy', 'hold' and 'sell' but you will also come across 'avoid' and 'take profits'.

This last category is often qualified with the advice to sell half your shares and keep the other half. The reasoning is that if the shares fall back after a good run you have at least banked some profits at the top of the market. If the shares continue to rise, then you are still getting some benefit from the ones you hung on to.

One drawback with newspaper tips is that there is a fixed space available each day so a set number of companies will be covered irrespective of whether news and events justify the selection.

Also, share prices for companies tipped in the papers can move substantially immediately the stock exchange opens so you may not be able to trade at the recommended price. This is particularly important if you ask your stockbroker to buy at best price – you may find yourself paying rather more than you intended, as traders have got in before you and bid the price up.

# Chapter 19
## Jargon Busting

Every way of life has its own language and the stock market is no exception. I have tried in this book to keep explanations as simple as possible but there are some often used expressions that are worth learning about.

In particular, you will see name tags attached to shares:

- *Blue chips*
  The largest companies on the stock market. The term is often used about any company in the FTSE 100.

- *Recovery stocks*
  Shares that have taken a battering but could be turning the corner, perhaps because of new management or improving markets.

- *Cyclical stocks*
  Companies that see their fortunes rise and fall with cycles in the economy. As the economy slows, theirs are the products that consumers can most easily manage without. Examples would be furniture retailers and leisure groups. Transport groups could suffer as fewer goods are moved and fewer people travel to work.

- *Counter-cyclical stocks*
  These companies do well out of a recession but are abandoned in the good times. A budget clothing retailer would expect to sell more when people are out of work but most of us prefer something stylish to wear when we go out to celebrate a pay rise.

- *Defensive stocks*
  These companies expect their share price to hold up well when shares prices are falling. Supermarkets should survive a downturn because we still have to eat.

- *Growth stocks*
  Small companies that are growing strongly and are expected to continue to do so.

- *Value stocks*
  Companies whose shares are cheap given their excellent prospects.

- *Penny stocks*
  Shares that have fallen below 10p on the stock market.

- *Shells*
  Companies that have cash but do not have any operating companies.

## Those pesky animals

### Bulls and bears

Most people have heard of bulls and bears, the most popular exhibits in the stock market zoo:

- Bulls are the optimists, the ones who buy shares in the touching belief that the good times will roll for ever and a day. If you think shares will go up, you are a bull.

- Bears are the gloomy pessimists, the Victor Meldrews who see the end of the world rapidly approaching. If you think shares will go down, you are a bear.

You can mix and match your animal instincts. You may be bearish about the market as a whole but bullish about an individual company or vice versa.

### Stags

While bulls and bears abound freely, stags have been almost hunted to extinction. A stag buys newly issued shares with the intention of selling for a quick profit. They were a protected species under

Margaret Thatcher, who fed them on a rich diet of privatisation issues.

The theory is that when a company is floated on the stock market it will be priced just below its real value. This (it is hoped by the financial advisers) avoids the ignominy of new issues dropping heavily as soon as they are released. As the shares gently rise in value, the advisers bathe in the healthy glow of a successful flotation and a large fee.

Stags attempt to spot when the advisers under-price the share issue. They apply for shares then sell in the market at a substantially higher price.

Alas, most new share issues are placed with institutional investors because that is cheaper than offering them all round. By sounding out how many shares institutions are willing to take and at what price (this is called *book running* or *book building*) it is possible for the shares to be placed at a realistic price.

All in all, the opportunities for stagging are few and far between for private investors.

## Dead cat bounce

Better to be a stag than a cat, the unfortunate creature that features in the dead cat bounce. Squeamish readers and cat lovers should look away now.

If you went to the top of a very tall building and dropped a dead cat over the edge it would hit the ground with such force that it would bounce, though not very high and it would immediately splat back onto the ground. Please do not try this at home and rest assured that the author has never conducted such an experiment with any creature, dead or alive.

When shares have fallen heavily, they often reach a point where they bounce up a little. This may be because shareholders who sold out at the top decide it is time to get back in or because new investors judge that the fall has gone far enough.

Alas, in dire circumstances the shares may well start falling again after a short pause. That short-lived minor recovery is known as a dead cat bounce.

## Case Study: HMV

It has been a long hard slog for music retailer HMV as competition from supermarkets and pirating have taken their toll. Various strategies over the years have failed, so that by 2011 the shares had sunk below 20p.

Chart 11: HMV

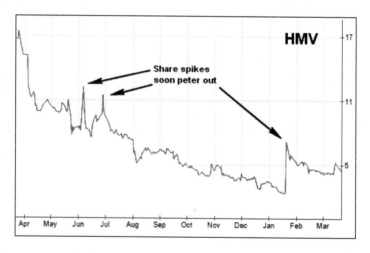

As the shares continued to slide throughout the year, there were two sharp upward spikes in June and another one appeared in January 2012. Unfortunately the problems had not gone away and the shares resumed their slide as reality prevailed. Each surge proved to be a dead cat bounce.

## Catching falling knives

A short walk from the menagerie to the kitchen takes us to the concept of catching falling knives. Sometimes the shares really do recover. It isn't a dead cat bounce after all.

Now the name of the game is to buy while shares are cheap and sell when they are dear. If you can catch a share after it has fallen heavily and hold it as it recovers you make a nice profit.

This is, however, a dangerous tactic, rather like trying to catch knives dropping from the top of the same building as the dead cat.

You might grab the handle, in other words catch a share that has been oversold and will recovery as soon as the panic is over.

On the other hand, you could grab the blade. You now own shares that keep falling. Snatching at falling shares is a dangerous business. They could be falling for a very good reason – the company could even be going bust.

## Case study: Barclays

The banking crisis that erupted in 2007 provided an object lesson in the dangers of trying to catch falling knives. As share prices in the sector tumbled across the board for two years, there were many occasions when investors could hope that all the bad news was finally out and a slump in share prices presented a chance to grab a bargain.

**Chart 12: Barclays**

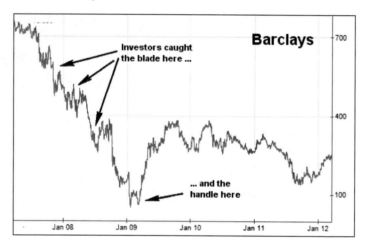

These respites in the downward spiral proved illusory as more woes emerged. It was not until a sharp fall in January 2009 that the worst was over for Barclays ... and this was one of the banks that escaped government control!

The reward for those who got their timing right was a quadrupling of the share price but even so the shares lost most of their gains before 2011 was out.

Even with hindsight it is difficult to see why one set of speculators got lucky when so many before had lost out.

# Chapter 20
## Rights Issues And Placings

I noted in chapter two that for the most part investors are buying shares on the secondary market: in other words, they are buying shares from other investors. There are occasions, however, where new shares are created and you need to know what action if any to take if a company in which you hold a stake creates new shares.

## Rights issue

When a company's shares are already traded on the stock market but it wants to raise more money, it may ask its current shareholders to stump up cash in return for extra shares. This is called a rights issue because the shareholders have the right to buy more shares if they want to.

It is only fair that existing shareholders are given the opportunity to buy because, as we shall see, rights issue shares are normally issued at a special low price.

Any rights issue proposed by the directors must by approved by a vote of ordinary shareholders at a special meeting. The right to buy shares will be conferred on shareholders who are on the share register on a specific date.

Under a rights issue the existing shareholders have the right to buy a set number of shares at a set price. Say the rights issue is 1-for-3 at 100p. That means you can buy from the company one new share for every three you already hold and you will pay 100p for each new share that you receive.

The cash goes to the company, usually for a specific purpose such as to make an acquisition or to reduce bank borrowings, but sometimes it is to provide cash in hand for day-to-day running costs or for future needs.

Be sure to read any documents the company sends you regarding a rights issue because in extreme cases the cash may be needed to stop the company going bankrupt.

### The discount

The good news about a rights issue is that the price of the new shares is usually set below the stock market price. After all, if you wanted more shares you could buy them on the stock market, so why on earth would you be tempted to pay the same price or more in a rights issue?

The difference between the rights issue price and the stock market price is called the discount (assuming that, as normal, the rights price is lower). If it is higher, then the rights issue is at a premium to the stock market price.

The size of the discount is decided by the company and it depends on several factors. The more shares on offer, the larger the discount is likely to be. A large discount is referred to as a deep discount.

If you are being asked to buy one new share for every one you already own, then you are being asked to double your stake, in which case you will need a strong incentive in the shape of a deep discount to persuade you to empty your pockets. On the other hand, if one new share is available for every 20 you already own, you may think the extra investment is a drop in the ocean and you will be asked to pay a figure close to the stock market price.

The size of the discount will also depend on how desperate the company is for the cash. If it is, in fact, a life saver because the company is in danger of going under then it will have to offer a very deep discount indeed to persuade the unfortunate shareholders to throw good money after bad.

There is a real skill in getting the rights price spot on. The price has to be low enough to tempt shareholders to pay up but high enough to raise the amount of cash that is needed.

## Underwriting a rights issue

You are not obliged to buy all or any of the shares offered to you in a rights issue. It is your right to buy, not your obligation. The rights issue may, therefore, be underwritten. This means that one or more stockbrokers or institutional investors have agreed to buy any shares scorned by the existing shareholders.

The underwriters will be paid a fee for their pains. After all, if the issue falls flat and few shareholders take up their rights then the underwriters will be forced to stump up the deficit. They could then be stuck with a large holding of shares that are difficult to sell.

If the company is confident of a good take-up by existing shareholders, it will not bother to have the rights issue underwritten, thus saving the cost of the underwriters' fees.

Shareholders in the company will probably be offered the opportunity to take more than their entitlement so that any rights not taken up can be distributed among those wanting extra. Otherwise any rights shares that are not applied for will be sold by the company through the stock market.

If you decline a rights offer and your entitlement is sold at a higher price than the rights price then the extra cash comes to you, minus the company's costs.

Say you are entitled to buy 1,000 shares at 100p each, that would cost you £1,000. If you forgo your rights and the shares are sold on the stock market at 150p each, the sale will raise £1,500. The company takes the £1,000 it wanted in the first place and passes the £500 'profit' to you.

It may seem a great idea to be offered cut-price shares but rights issues are not universally popular with shareholders. You may have made as big an investment as you felt comfortable with and now you are being asked to put up more cash that you may not have readily available.

Also, when a company makes a rights issue the share price tends to fall to some point between the existing share price and the rights price, so you see the value of your shareholding reduced.

## Placing and open offer

Instead of giving existing share holders the right to buy new shares, a company may offer new shares to institutional investors. This is called a placing. Since the existing shareholders are being bypassed, they will be asked to approve this arrangement, just as they would be required to vote on a rights issue.

There are several benefits, from the company's point of view, of making a placing rather than a rights issue. First of all, it costs much less. The lower the costs of making the issue, the more of the proceeds go into the company coffers.

Offering shares to a handful of institutions, each taking a large batch of shares, is a good deal cheaper, not to mention faster, than writing to all the shareholders and allocating small parcels of shares to all those who take up the rights.

There is a greater degree of certainty in a placing. The company may already know of institutions wanting to invest.

The placing price can be decided by the company or set through what is known as book building or book running. Institutions and stockbrokers will be asked how many new shares they are prepared to take and what price they are prepared to pay, so demand for shares, and the highest price that they can be sold for, is judged more accurately than taking a guess in a rights issue.

Often, though not always, a placing is accompanied by an open offer. This means that shareholders can apply to buy some of the shares being issued in the placing. They will pay the same price per share as the institutions.

## Bonus issues and share splits

There are two other circumstances in which new shares are created but in these cases the shares are allocated automatically to the existing shareholders without payment. They tend to happen when shares are rising strongly; and as a consequence they almost disappeared after the market fell heavily in the wake of the credit crunch.

### Bonus issues

Under a bonus issue, as with a rights issue, existing shareholders will be allocated one or more shares for every so many already held. The norm is for one new share for every four or five held, although the exact proportion can vary.

Because shareholders do not have to pay anything, there is no need to apply for bonus shares. As with a rights issue, there will be a specific date on which the bonus issue will apply. Shareholders on the share register on that date get the bonus issue.

Bonus issues are usually made when a company has been trading particularly well and they frankly serve no real purpose except to provide a psychological boost by flagging up the good performance. The share price will fall in proportion to the size of the bonus issue. If you get one extra share for every five held then the share price will fall by roughly one fifth, leaving your total holding worth the same amount.

### Share splits

In a share split the effect tends to be more dramatic. As with a bonus issue, you get extra shares free but this time you usually get far more. At the very least your shares will be split in two, so you end up with twice as many shares. If the shares are split into five you will have five shares for each one you held previously.

Again, as with the bonus issue, the share price on the stock market is likely to fall accordingly so your total holding will be worth roughly the same.

Share splits are usually introduced after a long upward run in the share price. In this country we tend to prefer share prices somewhere between 100p and 1,000p, in contrast to the US, Europe and Japan where you have fewer but more highly priced shares.

The thinking is that cheaper shares are more marketable. Shareholdings can be sold in smaller batches and the total price will not be so daunting for small shareholders.

This is complete nonsense. If you want to sell part but not all of your shareholding in a company you can split a batch of 100 shares into two parcels of 50 just as easily as you can split a batch of 1,000 shares into two parcels of 500 each, or 10,000 into two lots of 5,000 each.

What splitting the shares does do is to swell the size of the share register, making it more expensive to maintain. For this reason some smaller companies have resisted the convention. Those that have happily allowed their shares to rise well above 2,000p without any obvious signs of indigestion include SABMiller, Johnson Matthey, Jardine Matheson, Royal Dutch Shell, AstraZeneca and British American Tobacco.

As with a bonus issue, a share split is usually a great psychological boost as it normally signals to the market that all is well, indeed extremely well. So while splitting the shares into, say, five should in theory reduce the price of the shares to a fifth of their former value, in practice they are likely to settle a little higher.

Companies making bonus issues or share splits will not want to suffer the ignominy of seeing the shares fall below the theoretical new price so the directors will be pretty confident about the immediate future for the company.

## Case study: Greggs

Bakery chain Greggs enjoyed many years of success after finding a profitable niche in the High Street. It developed a knack of producing popular new products and having established itself in the lunchtime market with a range of sandwiches it repeated the feat with bacon sandwiches for those who eat breakfast on the way to work.

Greggs simply ignored the relentless rise in its share price as it topped £20 in the stock market recovery after the post-millennium crash. Even as the market generally subsided from 2008 onwards, Greggs went from strength to strength, paying a rising dividend for more than 20 consecutive years and at one point propelling the share price above £40.

Eventually, Greggs decided that it would split its existing shares into ten new ones, a decision announced alongside annual results in March 2009. At that point the shares traded at around £36.

The results themselves were unspectacular: pre-tax profits were down 7.8% in what had been a difficult year of rising prices for energy and ingredients. However, chief executive Ken McMeiken provided a psychological boost by raising the dividend total by 6.4% and revealing a share split to take place a couple of months later.

Greggs shares edged higher to £38 by the time the split came into force, giving a theoretical price of 380p for the new shares. However, they soon moved up to 394p, effectively a gain of 14p a share.

Our table shows what happened to holdings of 1,000 shares before and after the share split:

Table 20: example share split

| | No of shares held | Market price | Value of holding |
|---|---|---|---|
| Before share split | 1,000 | 3800p | £38,000 |
| After share split | 10,000 | 380p | £38,000 |
| After share price gain | 10,000 | 394p | £39,400 |

# SECTION E
## Takeovers

# Chapter 21
## Mergers And Acquisitions

Takeovers are arguably the most exciting aspect of stock market investing because it is one way that investors can make substantial profits in a short space of time. Newspapers love takeovers because they often involve companies with colourful personalities as chief executive; so there is generally plenty of press coverage, which means shareholders can easily keep themselves aware of any developments.

It is quite likely that at some stage you will invest in a company that is subsequently involved in a takeover or a merger (a merger is when two companies join together to become one). This activity is referred to as mergers and acquisitions, more often than not abbreviated to M&A.

Takeovers may be:

- Friendly: a friendly bid is where the two sides agree on a price and the target company recommends its shareholders to accept.

- Hostile: in a hostile bid, the target company tries to fight off the bidder and advises its shareholders to reject the offer.

### Takeovers and share prices

In takeovers, the share price of the target company tends to rise, sometimes even before the bid is announced. This may happen because news of an approach leaks out or because investors sense that a particular company is susceptible to an offer. Since investors privy to inside information can make large profits from buying shares before a bid is announced, the procedure is governed by a strict Takeover Code. Bidders believe that takeovers create the opportunity to increase sales or cut costs, which is why they are usually willing to pay a *bid premium,* that is they offer more than the prevailing market price. The share price of a bidding company often falls as its shareholders fret over whether it is paying too high a premium.

Although takeovers can happen at any time, they are understandably more prevalent when shares are comparatively cheap. A surge of takeover activity can be a sign that the stock market is rising again after a fall; similarly the sudden drying up of takeovers can signal that the stock market has peaked.

### Do takeovers work?

Opinions vary on whether takeovers really work. Among the most spectacular successes was Hanson, built into a transatlantic conglomerate giant in the 1980s by an astute strategy of buying undervalued companies.

On the other hand, some boards seem merely to want to flex their muscles in a show of strength or they have run out of ideas for growing the businesses they already have. Takeovers can end up destroying rather than creating value, although that is all too often forgotten when the next wave of takeovers comes along.

One group of people always gain in a takeover situation, whatever the outcome. An army of highly paid advisers drawn from each company's lawyers, stockbrokers, financial advisers and PR experts pore over all the details at great and expensive length.

## Takeovers

In a takeover, one company buys another. We shall refer to the company making the bid as the bidder and the company on the receiving end as the target company. The bidder is also referred to as the *offeror* and, less formally in the press, as a *predator* or a *suitor.*

The majority of takeovers and mergers involve companies in the same line of business. This is known as a trade deal. These deals are popular because there are advantages in putting two companies with complementary businesses together.

It may be possible to grow the combined businesses by selling goods and services to each other's customers or by creating a nationwide business instead of two regional ones. Working together to boost sales is known as synergy.

There could also be cost savings, for example from combining the sales staffs or from putting manufacturing facilities under one roof. This is cost cutting – although companies will often refer to it as synergy because this sounds better than saying staff will be fired to save money.

If the bid is from a company outside the sector it is referred to as a financial bid. In this case there are no synergies to be achieved as the businesses cannot be combined, although it may be possible to boost sales through more dynamic management. The bidder will probably be hoping to make the operations more profitable by cutting costs.

### Takeover Panel

Where one company buys, or attempts to buy, another company, the procedure is governed by a strict set of rules called the Takeover Code and is supervised by the Takeover Panel.

Takeover rules have been tightened considerably over the years for the good of all investors.

The Takeover Panel has 34 members, including representatives of professional bodies such as the Association of British Insurers, the British Bankers' Association, the Confederation of British Industry and the Institute of Chartered Accountants in England and Wales.

This is not a cosy Old Boys' club, nor is it a protection racket to preserve the rights of City bigwigs. It has developed a justified reputation for fairness and even handedness. It does not flinch from bringing large quoted companies and their City advisers to book in order to ensure fairness for all, including small shareholders. The Takeover Panel expects the spirit of the Code to be followed as well as the letter of the law.

The Takeover Code has been developed since 1968, not only to promote fairness but also to ensure that takeovers and takeover battles are conducted in an orderly fashion. Its rules apply even before a bid is formally launched and it governs not only the companies involved in the bid but all their advisers.

The code does not rule on whether a takeover is set at a fair price or makes commercial sense. That is a matter for the shareholders to decide.

You can read the full details of the extensive and thorough code by logging on to the Takeover Panel's website (**www.thetakeoverpanel.org.uk**) – the relevant web page is:

**www.thetakeoverpanel.org.uk/wp-content/uploads/2008/11/code.pdf**

In the next two chapters we shall pick out the main points that affect small shareholders.

## Mergers

In a merger, two companies agree to come together to form a new group. A new company will be set up and shareholders in both existing companies will receive new shares in the new group in place of their existing holdings.

The size of the allocations will depend on the sizes of the respective companies that are merging. Assuming that both companies are quoted on the stock exchange, the ratio will be broadly in line with their market capitalisations.

# Chapter 22
## Before A Bid

A bid can be brewing for many months before it is formally announced. Sometimes talks are held and the bidder walks away only to return with new proposals when it feels that the target company will be more receptive.

These informal talks, out of the glare of publicity, can be very useful in determining whether it is worth pursuing a potential bid or in negotiating terms acceptable to all parties.

Time was when companies refused to comment on market rumours but nowadays the Takeover Panel requires them to issue statements when the market gets wind of a potential bid, which is quite often.

### When companies must issue a statement

Although it is not necessary to comment on a rumour that is utterly without foundation, target companies must own up if a firm offer has been received, or there is untoward movement in the share price after an undisclosed approach has been received or when negotiations are taking place.

There is no specific ruling about how untoward a movement in the share price has to be. It used to be 10% but a more flexible approach is taken these days and companies tend to err on the side of revealing all when their shares move sharply upwards.

A company cannot be wrong in making an announcement but it can regret keeping quiet and subsequently having to admit it has been hiding an approach. If in doubt, companies can consult the Takeover Panel, which leans on the side of making an announcement if it is in the interests of shareholders.

The bidder must put any proposal to the board of the target company before it makes it a public pronouncement. That is not only courtesy, it gives the target company's directors a chance to assess the proposal and decide on what stance to take.

Getting the two sides together at an early stage, before any announcement is made, can be advantageous to shareholders. It means that the share price of the target company is not distorted by the announcement of an approach that has no chance of success. On the other hand, it gives the target company the opportunity to try to persuade the bidder to offer a higher price.

At this stage there is no obligation on either side to make a public announcement. It is impossible to say how many approaches are never revealed but it is likely that they are heavily in the majority.

### When news of a takeover bid leaks out

Inevitably, though, word of an approach sometimes leaks out. It shouldn't, and it is against the Code, but it happens. The manifestation of the leak comes in a sharp rise in the shares of the target company. When that happens, the target company is obliged to reveal the approach.

This is usually done by issuing an anodyne and fairly vague statement along the lines that an approach has been received that may or may not lead to an offer; the approach is very preliminary and there is no guarantee that a bid will be made.

Occasionally matters are at a more advanced stage. The target company may be able to say that it is in discussions with the potential bidder and possibly indicate a proposed price per share.

An approach can be tentative or an outright threat or anywhere in between.

At the most tentative level, a predator and target company will simply be having preliminary talks with no proposal of any kind on the table.

## Pre-conditional offer

The next level up is a pre-conditional offer. The predator has put forward a proposal in principle but there are conditions to be met before this is turned into a firm offer. These conditions usually include the right to look at the target company's accounts in confidence, referred to as carrying out due diligence, and it may still be necessary for the predator to raise enough finance to pay for the bid. Pre-conditional offers are often rejected out of hand by the target company as being too vague.

## Indicative bid

Somewhere in the middle of the scale in an indicative bid. The predator indicates the price it intends to offer for the target company's shares.

Indicative bids may be rejected by the directors of the target company. You will often see phrases such as 'seriously undervalues the company and its prospects'. It is the duty of the target company's board, in the interests of their shareholders, to try to drive the bid price as high as possible.

Indicative bids are frequently dismissed as opportunistic, a pretty meaningless term, since every bid is made because someone sees an opportunity.

## Firm offer

At the top end of the scale is a firm offer. The predator has finance available and has put forward a bid price. This has to be taken seriously by the target company although the offer can still be rejected as too low.

These announcements would normally come from the target company but the predator may sometimes make an announcement even if no bid is yet on the table. This could be to state an intention to make a bid if finance can be raised, or it could be a decision not to bid after all.

If a predator rules out making a bid it cannot then make an offer for at least six months except in special circumstances. The main exceptions are if another predator makes an offer or if the target company agrees to submit to a firm bid.

## Offer period

A company may be deemed to be in an offer period even before a formal proposal is put forward, provided a serious possibility of a bid has arisen.

During an offer period all shareholders holding more than 1% of the shares in the target company must announce any share purchases or sales they make. Directors in the target company are barred from dealing in the shares.

The company is also obliged to make far more disclosures of all its activities, day-to-day matters than it would normally not have to tell the stock exchange about. This is to ensure nothing affecting the bid is hidden.

Takeovers are time consuming for the company secretary, who has the unenviable task of issuing all the information. They are also expensive for the potential bidder, which will be paying advisers to assist in evaluating any bid.

## Put up or shut up

To stop the whole process rolling on indefinitely, with the target company distracted from its day-to-day business, the Takeover Panel introduced a deadline by which a potential bidder must make a decision on whether to bid or not. This is known as a put up or shut up ruling.

It allowed target companies to request that a potential bidder should be ordered to 'put up or shut up' within six to eight weeks, which was regarded as adequate time to get finance in place and decide on an offer price.

This rule was enforced when US food group Kraft bid £12 billion for UK confectionary manufacturer Cadbury, but the outrage over a foreign company grabbing a national treasure prompted a further tightening of the rules in 2011.

Now any company revealing that it has received an approach must name the potential bidder and the put up or shut up timetable starts rolling automatically at this point, which takes the onus off target companies of having to request a ruling. The grace period has been shortened to 28 days.

Target companies can, however, ask for the period to be extended if talks are bearing fruit and there is a genuine possibility that a bid will be forthcoming that is in the interests of the target company's shareholders.

If the predator chooses to walk away, it cannot bid for six months unless an alternative bid emerges from another bidder.

## Mandatory offers

One key rule of the Takeover Code is that if a major shareholder buys more shares and its stake rises above 30% it is obliged to make a bid for all the rest of the shares. The aim is to spare minority shareholders from getting locked into a company where a large shareholder has gained control.

A mandate is a command. Do not be confused by the way that politicians misuse the word to mean permission. A mandatory offer is one that must be made.

The bid must be at least equal to the highest price that the bidder has paid for shares during the previous 12 months.

You may wonder why 30%. After all, you need just over 50% to gain full control of a company. With more than half the shares you can then outvote all the rest of the shareholders put together.

However, it is possible for a large shareholder to gain effective control of a company with less than 50%. If one shareholder has 45% of a company and the rest of the shares are divided among a large number of holdings, it is highly unlikely that the small shareholders would be able to band together as an opposing force.

In any company there are always shareholders who fail to vote at all while many more slavishly back the existing board.

Stock exchanges in various parts of the world have considered at what level a major shareholder is likely to take effective control. Any figure is inevitably arbitrary but it is there to protect small shareholders.

The Australian Stock Exchange settled on 20% as the threshold. That does seem, though, to be rather on the low side. London chose 30% as a fair compromise.

## Substantial acquisition rules

Potential predators are restricted in the number of shares they can buy before they launch a full bid.

This may seem a bit unfair on the predator but the rule protects shareholders in the target company who might otherwise sell in the market at a lower price without realising something is afoot.

The rule also restricts predators that are seeking to build a sizeable stake without making a bid.

It is perfectly permissible for a predator to buy one large stake of any size in the target company, bearing in mind that going above 30% automatically sparks a mandatory offer to all shareholders at the same price or better. A large shareholder seeking to get out may be only too happy to part with a slab of shares at one go. Dribbling a large holding out into the market drives the price progressively lower.

Predators buying from more than one source cannot buy a total of more than 10% of the target company within a seven day period if that takes them above 15%. This rule is waived if the predator announces an intention to make a bid.

If the share buying takes the predator above 30%, then a bid is mandatory anyway.

## Inducement and break fees

Another change that was made when the takeover rules were tightened in 2011 was the banning of:

- **inducement fees,** under which the target company paid some or all of the predator's costs in launching a bid, and

- **break fees,** where the target company paid the bidder's costs if an agreed bid failed because a better offer was forthcoming from another bidder.

These fees were previously permitted on the grounds that they might encourage a bid that was to the advantage of the target company's shareholders. They were always controversial because it was a moot point whether it was right for a company to pay the bidder's costs as well as its own.

## Due diligence

Bidders naturally want to be quite sure the target company is in good health and they will ask to be allowed to carry out due diligence.

Assuming that the proposed takeover is a friendly one, this is no problem and the target company will allow the bidder to take a detailed look at its accounts (also called looking at the books).

The general financial health of the target company will be pretty well known because it can be gleaned from the twice-yearly results statements the company is required to release.

However, companies hold back data that they consider to be commercially sensitive, information that they think would help the rivals they are competing against in the marketplace.

Accountants, legal experts and other consultants for the predator will sign undertakings not to divulge any secrets before being allowed to look at information such as the terms of bank loans, contracts with customers, tenancy agreements, employment contracts and other minutiae that could have an impact on the value of the business.

The process can be expensive if those highly paid consultants are poring over the books for several weeks. They will be looking for ways to boost sales or, more likely, to save money by cutting out duplicated costs.

Due diligence is a bit tricky when the bid is hostile, since the target company will be reluctant to allow an unfriendly bidder to see its innermost secrets, especially if the approach has come from a rival.

## You must be serious

Any person, company or institution launching a bid has got to be able to see the bid through. Any potential bidder must, therefore, disclose its financial position to ensure that if every shareholder in the target company accepts the offer there is enough cash to buy them all out.

The bidder must also disclose all fees relating to the deal that it is paying to its advisers and it must give detailed information of its intentions regarding the employees of the target company.

These rules were tightened after the Kraft takeover of Cadbury, partly because Kraft indicated that it would save the Cadbury factory at Keynsham, near Bristol, that was due to close, only to backtrack after the bid went through.

# Chapter 23
## A Bid Is Launched

A takeover bid is generally good news if you hold shares in the target company but is usually not particularly welcome for shareholders in the predator company.

That is because takeovers are normally pitched at a higher level than the stock market price of the target company. This is known as the bid premium. There is no obligation to pay a bid premium, but if a bidder is keen to buy then it is usually willing to up the ante in order to succeed.

Bidders prefer to get the backing of the target company's board. If they do, then it is an agreed or recommended bid.

An agreed bid has a greater chance of success, since the target company's board is urging its own shareholders to accept. The offer has to be sufficiently generous to win this recommendation.

If the target company rejects the approach, the bidder may still go ahead and launch a hostile bid. The terms still have to be attractive enough to tempt the target company's shareholders to accept. After all, you could sell on the stock market if you wanted to get out.

Hence shares in the target company will usually go up when a bid is announced.

Just occasionally a bid may be pitched below the stock market price. This can happen when a company finds itself in dire financial trouble and a rescuer emerges, but only at a lower price than the stock market was hoping for.

## Irrevocable acceptances

In an agreed bid, the directors of the target company will be accepting the offer for any shares that they own and it is possible that other large shareholders will agree to accept also.

It is quite usual in these circumstances for such acceptances to be binding. The backing of a sizeable number of shares, possibly even a majority of them, may be a crucial factor in persuading a predator to launch a bid.

The directors, and any other shareholders who have been privy to the negotiations, may make an irrevocable promise to accept the bid even if a better offer comes along. Alternatively, they may reserve the right to switch sides if a higher offer is made.

## Hostile bids

A bid can still be made even if it is rejected by the board of the target company. A spurned suitor can appeal directly to the target company's shareholders who, after all, own the company. This is known as going hostile.

A hostile bidder is entitled to obtain a copy of the target company's share register and to communicate with all the people who are on it.

The bidder will send documents setting out its arguments for taking over the company and urging the shareholders to accept. The target company will also write to its shareholders setting out the reasons for rejecting the offer.

If you own shares in a company that is the subject of a takeover offer it is in your interests to read these documents and to weigh up the arguments before deciding whether to accept or reject the offer.

## The offeror

Now let us consider bids from the point of view of investors in the offeror. Benefits are distinctly less obvious. Indeed, a bidding company may see its share price fall as investors worry about whether it is overpaying for the proposed acquisition.

Assuming that the bid succeeds, there will be immediate costs to pay over and above the price of buying the target company. If cash has been borrowed from the bank to fund the bid, then the interest bill will go up. Redundancies to remove duplication in the workforce will have to be paid for.

Management time will have to be spent in integrating the target company into its new owner and there may be additional costs in making the computer systems compatible or meshing the distribution networks.

The benefits, in contrast, take time to come through.

The bidding company will say when it announces its bid whether it expects the acquisition to be earnings neutral in the first year, that is when earnings per share for the group would be roughly the same with or without the acquisition.

If the bidder has struck a good bargain, the acquisition could be earnings enhancing from the start, in other words any costs will be immediately more than offset by the gains.

More likely than not, it will take some months, possibly even a couple of years, before the acquisition starts to show its full potential, in which case the takeover will initially be earnings dilutive, that is earnings per share will be reduced at first before rising in subsequent years.

## Bid terms

Any company making a firm bid must state the price per share that it is offering and must be certain that it has sufficient financial backing if it is offering cash.

The bidder can offer cash, some of its own shares or a combination of both in return for the target company's shares. It must clearly state its terms.

Individual shareholders in the target company are not obliged to accept an offer even if it is recommended by the company's own board. As we shall see later in this section when we discuss the bid timetable, it can be good tactics to hold off for a while. Do not be bullied into taking the offer immediately by the tone of the offer document that is sent out to the target company's shareholders.

Bids may be subject to conditions set by the bidder. If the acquisition is a large one, the bidder may need to seek the permission of its own shareholders to proceed. Where the takeover is between two similar companies it is usual for the bid to be conditional on not being referred to the Competition Commission or the European Commission, either of whom could block it as being against the public interest.

The bid will certainly be conditional on a minimum number of acceptances. This will normally be set at 50% plus one share, which gives a majority stake, but it can be higher, even as high as 90%.

Bidders often stipulate 90% acceptances as a condition when they launch the bid but reduce the level to 50% subsequently. They always have the right to waive, that is to drop, conditions but not to introduce new ones.

If and when all the conditions have been met or have been waived by the bidder, the bid will be declared unconditional, which means the takeover has succeeded. If all conditions are not met or waived then the bid fails and the bidder cannot make a new approach for at least 12 months.

## Compulsory share purchases

Where a company makes a bid and gains acceptances for at least 90% of the target company's shares, it is entitled to force the tiny remaining minority to accept the bid.

The bidder normally wants full control of the target company and having a few errant shareholders left in is a real nuisance. If that happens, separate accounts have to be drawn up for the target company and sent to the remaining shareholders.

At the same time, it is really not in your interests to be trapped into a company with just a handful of other tiny investors. You will be at the mercy of a massive shareholder who doesn't want you hanging around and you will not be able to sell your shares because they will have been delisted from the stock exchange.

On the other hand, if a sizeable minority of shareholders refuse to accept, it may be because the bid price was too low and in that case they are entitled to hang on and hope that they will be offered more at some time in the future.

So again, the 90% threshold may be an arbitrary figure but it is a reasonable level and it is there to balance the interests of all parties.

## Loan notes

Most bids come with a loan note alternative, that is, you can accept loan notes rather than cash to the value of your shareholdings.

A loan note is an IOU. You are letting the successful bidder hang on to the cash it owes you rather than taking the money for your shares immediately.

The reason for this alternative is that accepting a bid will usually create a capital gain and investors who have used up their capital gains allowance for the year will face a tax liability.

There is no capital gain on the loan note until you cash it in, so you can spread your gain over more than one tax year.

A set rate of interest will be paid on the loan notes, usually payable every six months. The issuer of the notes will let you cash them in on certain specified dates each year.

## Reverse takeovers

In most takeovers a large company takes over a smaller one. This is because the smaller company comes at a lower price and the larger company will either have enough cash to pay outright or it will be able to issue new shares without swamping its own existing shareholders.

The outcome of a reverse takeover may not be straightforward. If the takeover is paid for in shares in the bidding company rather than cash then the shareholders in the target company may actually end up with more than half the shares in the enlarged group.

The most common reason for a reverse takeover is a technical device to give a large unquoted company a stock market listing. So instead of the big company buying the little one and losing the listing, the quoted company bids for the larger unquoted company, paying in its own quoted shares rather than in cash. In such cases management of the larger company usually takes charge of the enlarged group.

## Scheme of arrangement

Instead of making a normal takeover offer, a predator may attempt to take control of a target company through what is known as a scheme of arrangement. These have been increasingly popular to the point that they are becoming the norm rather than the exception.

The biggest advantage for the bidder is that it is simpler and cheaper than an ordinary takeover. For one thing, it does not attract stamp duty and it can be a considerably faster process than a formal takeover.

Under a conventional bid, the predator is setting out to buy the shares of each shareholder individually. With a scheme of arrangement, the bidder is asking for permission to buy the entire company at one fell swoop.

Shareholders in the target company must vote on the deal and:

- Votes for at least 50% of the shares must be cast.

- At least 75% of the votes cast must be in favour.

Shares already owned by the bidding company are not counted.

A 51% acceptance is not good enough, as it is with an ordinary bid. The 75% rule is to protect the rights of small shareholders in the target company so they are not steamrollered into accepting.

Success means that any dissenters are overridden automatically and they must take the offer. It is not necessary to gain the support of 90% of the target company in order to force out the minority.

One disadvantage for the predator is that a scheme of arrangement is more vulnerable to a competing offer from another bidder. There is no point in the predator buying shares in the target company because these cannot be counted in the vote, so it is possible for a rival to buy enough shares in the target company on the stock market to block the arrangement.

A scheme of arrangement requires the support and cooperation of the board of the target company. This is because it is the target company, not the bidder, that actually puts the arrangements in place by calling an extraordinary general meeting of all its shareholders. It is also why this arrangement is often used when two companies are merging rather than one taking over the other.

Since the target company is supporting the offer, it is usual for the 75% hurdle to be cleared but that does not always happen if a concerted campaign can be waged against the deal.

## Partial offers and tender offers

It is possible for a predator to ask the Takeover Panel for permission to make a partial bid in which it will end up with a sizeable stake but less than 100% of the target company, and possibly less than the 30% level at which control is deemed to have been secured.

The partial offer can be in cash or in the bidder's own shares.

At least 50% of shareholders not connected with the bidder need to give their approval for a partial bid to go ahead.

These safeguards are to protect ordinary shareholders, who are at risk of getting locked into a company that has effectively been taken over without the bidder paying a premium for the privilege.

There are other restrictions. For instance, partial offers where the suitor ends up with more than 30% of the shares – the level at which it would normally be required to make a full bid – will not normally get the go-ahead from the Panel if the bidder has bought shares in the target company during the previous 12 months.

Also, if the predator intends to end up with between 30% and 50% of the target company it must declare the precise number of shares it intends to buy and it cannot declare the partial offer unconditional unless it secures that amount.

Shareholders should be wary of the possibility that the predator will make a full bid some time in the near future. If a full bid is made at a higher price than the partial offer, the shareholders who accepted the partial offer miss out on the difference.

The bidder may state that it does not intend to make a full bid. In that case it cannot bid for at least six months. Nor can it buy any more shares in the market for 12 months if the partial offer is successful.

Tender offers are cash only and the bidder must not end up with more than 30% of the target company.

The offer may be at a price fixed by the bidder. If the offer is oversubscribed, that is acceptances for more than the required number of shares are received, the acceptances are scaled down. For example, if a tender offer was made for 10% of a target company and shareholders accepted for 20% of the shares, each accepting shareholder would keep half their shares and sell the other half to the bidder.

The alternative is for the bidder to set the maximum price it is prepared to pay and for accepting shareholders to state the minimum price they are prepared to accept at or below that level.

If the tender offer is not fully taken up, then all accepting shareholders will get the maximum price stipulated by the bidder. If the offer is oversubscribed, then the strike price is set at the lowest level that fills the tender. All shareholders accepting at or below the strike price will receive the strike price for all the shares they tendered.

Bidders can stipulate a minimum acceptance level for the tender, so if very few shareholders accept the offer can be dropped. The minimum level is, though, quite low, usually 1% of the target company and in any case no more than 5%. This is to prevent a potential bidder from testing how the land lies without making a serious commitment.

## Stub equity

On rare occasions shareholders in a target company may be offered the opportunity of taking cash for most of their holdings while retaining a small stake in either the bidder or the target company, remaining as minority shareholders.

They are left with the 'stub' of their holdings, hence the name stub equity. The theory is that these shareholders get the best of both worlds. They receive a nice dollop of cash for most of their holdings but they still get some benefit if the target company does really well under its new owners.

The big advantage for the bidder is that less cash has to be found to fund the bid, since it is not buying all the shares.

Stub equity fell into disrepute donkey's years ago when a supermarket chain called Gateway (later resurrected as Somerfield) was the subject of a bid battle. A private equity firm by the fanciful name of Isosceles won by grossly overpaying. To cut the cost of its pyrrhic victory as best it could, Isosceles offered stub equity in the now debt-laden group.

The stub fell in value to the point where you couldn't give it away and nothing more was heard on the subject in this country for about 20 years until the notion was dragged up again in the takeover of property company Canary Wharf.

Offering stub equity may prove to be a sop to critics who argue that predators, particularly private equity companies, generate huge returns by taking companies private, loading them up with debt so they get their cash back, then refloating them on the stock market.

However, that raises the conclusion that they have underpaid in the first place. Shareholders accepting stub equity are locked in as minority shareholders in a company that is taken private so it may be very difficult to get the rest of their investment out until the company is refloated, possibly several years down the line.

## Competition regulators

However much you may welcome a takeover bid as an investor, there are regulators in the UK, Europe, the US and elsewhere who see things from a different angle. Their job is to ensure that putting two companies together does not leave too much power concentrated in too few hands.

In the UK, the Office of Fair Trading screens mergers and takeovers. Most are waved through but if the OFT has doubts it will refer the case to the Competition Commission for a more thorough investigation.

The Competition Commission used to be called the Monopolies Commission until jokes about 'why is there only one Monopolies Commission?' led to a name change.

The OFT referral will be based on whether a deal poses the threat of a substantial lessening of competition. There is no specific level, but if the two merging companies have more than 25% of a particular market between them the deal is likely to be referred.

The OFT may not be looking at the whole market. For example, when cruise lines Carnival and Royal Caribbean were fighting a bid battle for UK rival P&O Princess, the OFT did not consider the whole holidays market but simply whether either bidder would end up with a stranglehold on the cruise market.

The OFT may also consider whether a company will gain a monopoly within a particular region or even smaller area. For instance, it wants to see more than one supermarket and more than one betting shop in each town.

Competition Commission reports normally take up to six months to investigate, although this can be extended. The Commission reports its findings to the Secretary of State for Trade and Industry.

The minister must approve a merger or takeover if the Competition Commission rules that it should be allowed. However, the minister has a choice whether or not to accept a ruling against a merger or takeover.

Regulators in Europe and the US have the power to block a deal. While they will leave any purely UK combination of businesses to the OFT, they may intervene if international markets are affected.

# Chapter 24
## Bid Timetable

The Takeover Code sets out a timetable designed to create an orderly procedure and to allow all parties adequate opportunity to safeguard their positions without letting the proceedings drag out for an undue length of time.

The offer document spelling out all the relevant details must be posted to the target company's shareholders within 28 days of the announcement of a definite offer. Initially the offer will then be open for at least 21 days to allow time for shareholders in the target company to accept if they wish to do so.

The target company's board is obliged to write to its own shareholders setting out its opinion of the merits of the bid and is expected to advise acceptance or rejection of the bid, giving its reasons. This advice can be changed if circumstances change, for example if the bidder raises its offer or a new bidder emerges.

The bidder can allow the bid to lapse at the first closing date. In other words it can scrap the bid and walk away after the 21 days are up. Alternatively, the bidder can extend the acceptance period but if the bid is not wholly unconditional 60 days after the offer document was sent out then the bid has failed.

If a rival bid is made part way through the bid timetable, the timetable will start again.

Where a bid fails, the bidder cannot launch a new bid for at least 12 months except under certain conditions. These are if the directors of the target company recommend a new offer or if another firm bidder emerges for the target company.

Table 20: takeover timetable

| Day | Event |
|---|---|
| Day 0 | The day that the bidder posts documents to shareholders in the target company. |
| Day 14 | The last day on which the target company's board can advise shareholders whether to accept the bid. If the advice is to reject the bid, then the document setting out the reasons, known as the defence document, must be issued by this date. |
| Day 21 | An offer must remain open for acceptances for at least 21 days to give shareholders in the target company reasonable time to make up their minds. This is the first closing date and the bidder can drop the offer at this point, declare the bid unconditional if it already has enough acceptances, or extend it for two weeks. |
| Day 35 | If the offer was declared unconditional as to acceptances on Day 21 then the offer can be closed at this point as the waverers have now had ample time to accept. |
| Day 39 | If the bid is hostile and it has not yet gone unconditional, this is the last date on which the target company can issue further information bolstering its defence. |
| Day 42 | Any shareholder who has already accepted an offer can withdraw that acceptance after this point. The idea is to allow shareholders the opportunity to switch sides if a better offer comes along. |
| Day 46 | The last date on which the bidder can raise its offer. Shareholders in the target company now have 14 days in which to take a final decision on whether to accept. |
| Day 60 | It's D-Day. Either the bidder has enough acceptances to declare the bid unconditional as to acceptances or that's the end of the story for another 12 months. No more extensions are allowed. |
| Day 81 | Any other outstanding conditions must be fulfilled or waived by this day so the offer can go fully unconditional. |
| Day 95 | The bidder must pay up within 14 days of the offer going fully unconditional so this is the last day to settle up. |

## Competing bidders

If you are really lucky, two or more bidders will compete to buy your company. In this case the bidding will escalate as each bid tops the previous one.

## Accelerated bids

Where there is a bid auction and the rivals keep making progressively higher bids there is a danger of the process dragging on for an inordinately long time, since the bid timetable goes back to Day 0 every time a new offer document is posted.

To speed up the process, the Takeover Panel may hold an accelerated auction in which the rivals put forward competing bids over several days rather than weeks until one bidder outbids the rest.

# Chapter 25
## Management Buyouts

Instead of a takeover by an external company, companies may be bought by a team of managers who take the company private. In other words, the company continues as a separate entity but it withdraws its stock market quotation.

The offer to buy all the shares may come from the exiting executives of the target company. This is known as a management buyout (MBO) because the existing management is buying out all the other shareholders. The logic behind this type of deal is that no-one should understand a company better than its managers – if they think the company is undervalued in the market they might be tempted to launch an MBO.

Sometimes the offer comes from a set of managers who are unconnected to the company and who think they can run it better than the existing executives. This is known as a management buy-in.

Very rarely, the proposed new team comprises some existing and some new executives – which a City wag dubbed as a bimbo (or buy in/management buy out).

All these situations are nowadays generally referred to as MBOs and we shall use this term irrespective of where the new bosses are coming from.

The management will almost certainly be getting financial backing from another source unless one of them is very rich. Banks may provide a loan or, more likely, venture capitalists are providing the cash.

Venture capitalists are groups of wealthy individuals who – among other activities – specialise in buying companies that they feel are undervalued by the stock market, so the immediate suspicion with any MBO is that someone is trying to get your company on the cheap.

Existing management should know the company inside out and if they see hidden value there, shareholders are entitled to wonder why that value has not been unlocked for the benefit of all shareholders already.

Those directors who are not going to be involved in the company after it has been taken private are referred to as independent directors. They will usually be the non-executives. Their role will be to represent the existing shareholders in the target company and not to side with any executives involved in the offer.

Since the independent directors have nothing to gain from the MBO – indeed, they will be losing their directorships and the fees they are paid – they can attempt to extract as high a bid as possible on behalf of the ordinary shareholders.

Some independent directors are rather better at this than others and there have been occasions where they have dug their heels in and refused to recommend acceptance of an MBO.

On other occasions they may lack a little spine in standing up to the executives. They have, after all, sat round the same boardroom table month after month and may have too cosy a relationship to start fighting.

In these circumstances your fate is often in their hands.

One factor that may help is that if the managers try to get ownership of the company on the cheap it is possible that another bidder will step forward and offer more. Don't count on it, but it does happen.

Another possibility is that major shareholders may revolt and vote down the MBO at an EGM even when it is recommended by the independent directors.

# APPENDIX

# Useful Websites

## Organisations

Association of Investment Companies – **www.theaic.co.uk**

Association of Private Client Investment Managers and Stockbrokers – **www.apcims.co.uk**

Financial Services Authority – **www.fsa.gov.uk**

London Stock Exchange – **www.londonstockexchange.com**

Takeover Panel – **www.thetakeoverpanel.org.uk**

## Free and subscription sites

ADVFN – **www.advfn.com**

BBC – **www.bbc.co.uk**

Citywire – **www.citywire.co.uk**

InvestEgate – **www.investegate.co.uk**

MoneyAM – **www.moneyam.com**

Morningstar (including Hemscott) – **www.morningstar.co.uk**

Motley Fool – **www.fool.co.uk**

Reuters – **www.reuters.co.uk**

Sharescope – **www.sharescope.co.uk**

# Index

# Great savings on Rodney Hobson's other books

As a buyer of *Shares Made Simple* you can order discounted print and eBook editions of all Rodney Hobson's titles. Simply go to:

**www.harriman-house.com/readeroffer/sharesmadesimple2**

or point your smartphone at the QRC below.

**www.harriman-house.com**

# Dividend Investor

*A practical guide to building a share portfolio designed to maximise income*

Rodney Hobson, author of bestseller *Shares Made Simple*, is back with a brand new book designed to help you build a balanced share portfolio that provides dividend income, whether you're just starting out or ready to retire.

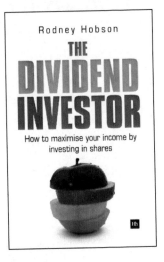

Rodney Hobson

THE
DIVIDEND
INVESTOR

How to maximise your income by investing in shares

Dividends - the distribution of part of a company's earnings to shareholders, usually twice a year - can be a valuable income stream for anyone. Designed for longevity but particularly pertinent in times of low interest rates, *The Dividend Investor* is packed with real-life examples and analysis of how to gain such added income through reliable shares with healthy dividends.

Topics made simple with Hobson's classic style include: ratios, yield, dividend cover, the dividend payout ratio, total return, cash flow, burn rate, gearing or leverage, interest cover, earnings per share and the price/earnings ratio. Plus the advantages and disadvantages of shareholder perks.

If you're looking to make the most from your investments, then this book is for you.

Paperback: 9780857190963
eBook: 9780857192349
**www.harriman-house.com/thedividendinvestor**

# How to Build a Share Portfolio

*A practical guide to selecting and monitoring a portfolio of shares*

## Effective share portfolios for the private investor

Running an efficient portfolio of shares means buying and selling the shares that make the most sense for you, and at the right time and price. Rodney Hobson, author of the bestselling *Shares Made Simple*, sets out how to do this without having to be a financial expert or full-time trader. Using plain language, he takes the reader simply and logically through the process, giving helpful examples and real-life case studies at every turn.

In *How to Build a Share Portfolio* you can:

- find out how to determine the right objectives for your portfolio
- learn how to pick shares that fulfill your investment ambitions, and when to drop those that no longer do so
- understand how best to set your portfolio's size and ensure it is diversified against risk
- discover the best ways of monitoring your portfolio, and of reducing losses and rebalancing it when necessary.

Anyone who is thinking of investing, however much or however little, will benefit from the information, advice and guidance contained in this book. Similarly, those who already have a portfolio will find it helps them to stand back and reassess whether they are making the most of their money and whether their portfolio is meeting their needs.

Paperback: 9780857190215
eBook: 9780857191236
**www.harriman-house.com/howtobuildashareportfolio**

# Small Companies Big Profits

*How to make money investing in small companies*

**Small is beautiful - if you have an eye for an opportunity.**

While most big fund managers and private investors seek the apparent safety of the largest stocks, the best investment ideas can be found among nearly 2,000 smaller companies whose shares are quoted on the London Stock Exchange.

This guide opens up a whole new world to investors, a world of solid companies that have found a profitable niche, ambitious start-ups with enormous growth potential and attractive takeover targets.

However, the risks match the rewards and the unwary investors need to learn how to spot the pitfalls and which companies are small because they do not deserve to grow.

**Small Companies**

**BIG**

**Profits**

How to make money
investing in small companies

Rodney Hobson

The book is packed full of case studies demonstrating the successes, failures and potential of small companies. Each succinctly presents the lessons to be learnt from their experience.

All investors looking to widen their portfolios will welcome this highly informative book covering an area of the stock market that is too often neglected by pundits, investors and the press.

Paperback: 9781905641789
eBook: 9780857191342
**www.harriman-house.com/smallcompaniesbigprofits**

# Understanding Company News

*How to interpret stock market announcements*

This book looks at company announcements, focussing on those issued through the London Stock Exchange by listed companies.

Almost all these announcements - such as annual results, share buying by directors, profit warnings and updates on current trading - are required under stock exchange rules or European Union directives. This book explains these rules and shows how to make sense of the announcements; enabling investors and others to take informed decisions.

**The book is divided into three sections:**

**Section A** looks at what the rules are, why they have been imposed and how they have evolved to give private investors a much fairer opportunity of competing with professional investors.

**Section B** lists and explains the routine statements that all companies issue on a regular basis: trading statements and profit figures. It tells readers what to look for, explains company jargon and shows how to read between the lines when all is not as well as it seems.

**Section C** considers important announcements, such as profit warnings and directors' share dealings, that are issued on an irregular basis as they arise. It explains which announcements are likely to affect the share price and why.

*Understanding Company News* is for all those baffled shareholders who throw communications from their companies straight into the bin and any investors who read company pronouncements but perhaps naively take everything they see at face value. And anyone working in related industries looking to untangle these company announcements will also find this book extremely valuable.

Paperback: 9781906659226
eBook: 9780857191328
**www.harriman-house.com/understandingcompanynews**